"It is not easy to figure ou̶ ̶.̶.̶.̶s beauti-
ful, tender guide, Tracey ̶ ̶.̶.̶.̶ u̶s do just that. With soulful stories,
grounding questions, and a realistic framework for how to move toward
figuring out what we want (and truly need), Gee reminds us that figuring
out our desires in this world is essential to helping make it a better one.
This book is meant to journey alongside you, so I hope you take notes,
write in the margins, and lean fully into the beautiful work found in these
pages. No matter who you are, no matter what season of life you find
yourself in, this book can help you ask the questions you've been waiting to ask—while finding the courage to explore the magic that shows
up along the way."

Kaitlin B. Curtice, award-winning author of *Native*,
Living Resistance, and *Winter's Gifts*

"I have been fortunate enough to benefit from Tracey's insightful guidance on my professional journey, and I am thrilled that her wisdom is
now accessible to a broader audience through *The Magic of Knowing What
You Want*. This book is a comprehensive toolkit designed to help you
navigate the intricate paths of ambition and self-doubt. With thought-
provoking questions, practical exercises, and inspiring personal stories,
it's an invaluable companion for anyone contemplating their future and
preparing to take their next leap."

Jennifer Alvarez, senior vice president of brand
and chief creative officer of the Miami Heat

"In this book, Tracey turns a scary question into a tender one, leading you
to an answer that may surprise you. As a generally self-assured person,
I was taken aback by how much I needed Tracey's teachings in this area,
her prompts for self-discovery, and her gentle nudge to dignify the desires
of our heart by committing to what makes us come alive. This book will
refresh a forgotten part of your soul. I'll be returning to it often."

Peace Amadi, PsyD, psychology professor and author
of *Why Do I Feel Like This?*

"In *The Magic of Knowing What You Want*, Tracey Gee leads the reader,
step-by-step, through a process that expands both horizons and hearts.
Let Tracey's deep questions 'read' your life—interpreting moments of joy

and pain, elation and disappointment—and you'll embark on a journey that connects you with your deep desires and heals your soul."

Bora Lee Reed, writer and communications director
of UC Berkeley's Goldman School of Public Policy

"I've always assumed that being one of the best in the world was something that naturally came to me. Reading this book gave me clarity on how all of my peak experiences were somehow aligned with my desires. It made complete sense why I was willing to work so hard to accomplish my goals. I will no longer ignore my desires in all aspects of life; I will instead acknowledge, explore, and embrace them!"

Lashinda Demus, 2012 Olympic gold medalist

"Tracey has an incredible gift of helping people identify and synthesize their strengths, gifts, and desires. In this book, she graciously gives voice to how common it is to not know what you want, and then walks you through some practical, creative, and accessible ways to get in touch with what your lived experiences have to say. Tracey has an abundance of expertise that she generously and masterfully shares in this book, and I could not recommend it enough."

Josh Green, coauthor of *What's Your Enneatype?*
An Essential Guide to the Enneagram

"Reading Tracey Gee's *The Magic of Knowing What You Want* was a profoundly affirming experience. Tracey's book made me feel deeply seen, and her personal stories and insights echoed my own experiences, making me realize that my desires can be validated and divinely inspired. This book is a must-read for anyone seeking to uncover the wisdom of their desires and live a life of deeper alignment and purpose. Tracey's heartfelt stories and profound insights have touched my heart and strengthened my resolve to live fully and authentically. I believe this book will inspire and guide many others to discover and embrace the magic of their own desires."

Brian Chung, cofounder and CEO of Alabaster Co

THE MAGIC
OF KNOWING
WHAT
YOU WANT

A PRACTICAL GUIDE TO UNEARTHING
THE WISDOM OF YOUR DESIRES

TRACEY GEE

Revell

a division of Baker Publishing Group
Grand Rapids, Michigan

Published by Revell
a division of Baker Publishing Group
Grand Rapids, Michigan
RevellBooks.com

Printed in the United States of America

Library of Congress Cataloging-in-Publication Data
Names: Gee, Tracey, 1974- author.
Title: The magic of knowing what you want : a practical guide to unearthing the
    wisdom of your desires / Tracey Gee.
Description: Grand Rapids, Michigan : Revell, a division of Baker Publishing Group,
    [2025] | Includes bibliographical references.
Identifiers: LCCN 2024018902 | ISBN 9780800746223 (paper) | ISBN
    9780800746834 (casebound) | ISBN 9781493448722 (ebook)
Subjects: LCSH: Self-actualization (Psychology) | Self-perception. | Affirmations. |
    Conduct of life.
Classification: LCC BF637.S4 .G447 2025 | DDC 158.1—dc23/eng/20240703

LC record available at https://lccn.loc.gov/2024018902

Cover design by Derek Thornton, Notch Design
Interior design by William Overbeeke

The names and details of the people and situations described in this book have been
changed or presented in composite form in order to ensure the privacy of those with
whom the author has worked.

The author is represented by the literary agency of Gardner Literary Agency.

Baker Publishing Group publications use paper produced from sustainable forestry
practices and postconsumer waste whenever possible.

25 26 27 28 29 30 31   7 6 5 4 3 2 1

This book is dedicated to you.
You deserve to be seen.

CONTENTS

INTRODUCTION

I never saw it coming. Unlike most people I knew, I had stayed in the same organization for my whole career, about twenty years, in large part because I loved the people I worked with. After dinner one evening at a conference, a colleague suggested I consider applying for a newly open VP role. I was aware of the opening but it hadn't crossed my mind to apply since becoming a VP would mean jumping two levels of the hierarchy. Upon a second look, however, I noticed how I'd been feeling restless for a new challenge. I recalled past internal interviews that had been empowering experiences even if they hadn't always landed me a new job per se, and I assumed this would be more of the same. The job was far from guaranteed, but I decided to apply anyway, motivated by the opportunity for learning and growth.

After submitting my application, I was surprised to find that I was excited. Every new role I'd ever considered up until that point had come with a fair share of ambivalence. Previously, I'd always been able to identify at least one negative for every positive about a potential new job, but this time, I was eager to find creative solutions for the challenges I saw, and it felt exhilarating. It felt odd, but in a good way, to feel so energized about making a change. I started to daydream about preparing for the interview and making a case for what I might bring to the table.

One evening, while I was chopping veggies for dinner, my phone blew up with a flurry of messages on a group work chat. We were discussing the scheduling of an unrelated upcoming meeting, but I realized some people on the thread were also making travel plans for job interviews. It dawned on me that the hiring process for the role I'd applied to was likely moving forward, too, but I hadn't heard anything. I grabbed my computer to check my email but found no new messages despite hitting the refresh button several times, even though I knew it didn't make sense to do so. I wanted to be optimistic, but I had to admit this was not a good sign. I'd known all along that the job wasn't a lock, but given my experience and contributions, I thought I'd at least get the chance to interview.

When I received the email a week later informing me I would not be moving forward in the selection process, I wasn't at all surprised but I was still devastated. As high as my excitement had been, the low was far lower. (For those who know what the Enneagram is, I once heard someone say you've never seen anybody as sad and dejected as an achievement-oriented type Three who has failed, and it was like they were describing me.) My friends told me they'd never seen me this way, and to be honest, neither had I.

I began to spiral as I started to question things. I questioned my assumption that I would spend the rest of my career in this organization and considered the terrifying notion of leaving. I questioned why a colleague (a white man with the same job title and experience as me) had been granted an interview when I hadn't, and why this made me feel terrible even if I was happy for him. I questioned why it didn't make me feel better when I asked for feedback about what I could have done to be a stronger candidate and was told nothing, that I was great but just needed "a few more years." Most of all, I questioned what to do next in response to all this, especially when one person told me it was my fault because I hadn't gamed my career the way men do, and according to them, I'd have to start playing those games if ever I wanted to get ahead. I questioned if being told for years that I was "a hidden treasure" wasn't the compliment it was intended to be and whether it was instead a nice-sounding way to say I wasn't being seen.

Having the process end unexpectedly and with opaque, conflicting narratives about why it had happened broke something in me in a way I didn't yet understand. A handful of people asked me to interview for other positions within the organization, giving me alternate possibilities to consider, but my heart wasn't in any of them. I listened to their pitches, but eventually I realized that moving through this crisis wasn't going to be as simple as throwing myself into a fresh pile of job descriptions and applications. I wasn't ready to move on. I had hit an all-time low in my life, and I needed to understand more about why this was taking me down so hard.

Forty Days of Desires

The question of what I wanted next loomed too large to have any kind of meaningful response. I was too depressed and confused to know what I wanted to do next week, much less for the next ten years. Any grand hope of creating a master plan for my life and career was laughable, the idea a nonstarter. So instead, I decided to start small. As a way to try something, *anything*, to take a step toward healing and feeling whole again, I created a personal experiment. I committed to doing one thing each day for forty days for no other reason than wanting to do it. The sole parameter I created was sincere wanting because, frankly, that was all I could muster. It felt like the babiest of baby steps, but it was something.

There was a small but insistent voice in the back of my mind that was critical of the endeavor and told me this had to be wrong somehow. It said spending that much time on myself and what I wanted was selfish, and I didn't know how to respond to this accusation. I had a hard time justifying the purpose of my experiment even if only to myself. There was no outcome tangible enough I could point to. Nothing approaching productivity. But I also didn't know what else to do. I was desperate, so I decided to try anyway.

During the first week, I decided to take my dog for a run at the beach. Since adopting her a couple months earlier, I'd thought about doing this several times, but it had always gotten pushed back for more urgent priorities, like meetings that needed to happen, projects that required attention, and errands that couldn't wait. That particular morning was cool and cloudy, and I wondered if I should postpone once again in favor of better weather, but something in my gut told me I should go anyway. So, after I loaded my dog in the car and grabbed her leash, we headed to the beach like we were on official business. When I got out of the car and saw the thick, grey marine layer, I wrinkled my nose, but being able to take deep breaths of the cool ocean air felt like a gift.

After running for a while, we came to a section of the strand where the beach walkway curves near an inlet to the marina, and I slowed to a walk. I saw some splashes in the water and assumed it to be seagulls. When I looked more intently, however, I realized that it was a dolphin, and not just one but two dolphins, swimming down the channel, gracefully rising and falling together in the water, coming up every so often to breathe, and then slipping back down below the water's surface.

Because of where they were in relation to where my dog and I stood on the path, we were so close, maybe only fifteen feet away. I turned my head to the side, looking for somebody else to marvel with, but the beach was empty. For a few magical moments, it was just us as we formed an unlikely congregation of creatures—human, canine, and marine.

I followed the dolphins as far as I could until the path ran out, and the pair eventually swam out of view, bringing the moment to an end. I was born and raised in California and grew up going to the beach every weekend; I've never experienced a dolphin sighting like this before or since. It felt sacred, almost like a divine affirmation of my little experiment and the exploration of a different way to be and heal. As happy, grateful tears fell down my cheeks, I told myself, *Maybe there's something here for me after all.* My lingering doubts dissipated, and I decided in that moment to do whatever I could to see the forty days through to the end. I felt I owed it to the dolphins.

So that's what I did. For forty days, I did something every day for no reason other than I genuinely wanted to, displaying a consistency that I surprised myself with. Most of what I chose to do was simple, like cooking a traditional Chinese dish my family loves (steamed fish with ginger, scallion, and soy sauce), trying a new facial mask and letting myself be still and breathe while it soaked into my pores, watching a rom-com for the fun of it, planting tomatoes, taking an afternoon nap, going for a hike but not rushing to get back, and reading books. I volunteered to be the parent chaperone for my son's first-grade class field trip to see a musical production of one of our favorite books, *Henry and Mudge*, and loved having the time with him and his classmates. I did a weekend girls' trip with my best friends. I rearranged the furniture in my office, attended a webinar, and wrote.

Without a model or guide for what to do, I was simply feeling my way through it, letting each day's desire take shape in a simple, unforced fashion. The entire experiment actually reminded me of what it felt like to play when I was young. One of my favorite memories as a kid was making mud cookies, the lesser-known cousin of mud pies. I prided myself on sourcing the best dirt and would pick out all the rocks to create as smooth and even a base as possible. I carefully mixed the water and soil to the right consistency so the mud wouldn't become too runny. I baked my muddy batter into neat rows of cookies on planks of scrap wood in the backyard until they hardened in the sun and looked nearly like the real thing. I loved feeling the elements of dirt, water, and sunlight on my hands. Of course, my efforts had no practical value. Those cookies didn't last. You certainly couldn't eat them. My mom couldn't even hang them on the fridge. But I loved making them for no other reason than the joy of creating just to create. After an afternoon of "baking," I would search for the nicest cookies of the batch to admire, whispering to myself, "Oh, this one is nice and even. It's one of the best ones," as I'd place it on a special plate.

That's how those forty days felt, like reclaiming a part of my childhood self that knew how to spend a sunny afternoon doing exactly what she wanted. But unlike her, I now also had my adult sensibilities about responsibility and productivity to contend with. Trying to reconcile those things left me feeling conflicted. It was hard to say how something like gardening, which I happen to be terrible at, mattered (because, sure enough, those poor plants suffered). What is *accomplished* by things like reading a book for pleasure or taking a nap? None of it felt noteworthy, dramatic, or impressive. Quite the contrary. It was small, everyday, and, one could argue, boring. All I knew was that it was *real*, allowing me to feel grounded and present to myself, and it seemed like that should carry some weight, despite me not being able to say what it was all for.

When the experiment ended, I told myself it was a nice thing to have done for myself; it had been a generally positive experience but not a lot to write home about. If it were a new restaurant that I tried for the first time, I'd have said it was pleasant but nothing special, and I probably wouldn't go back. But now, with the 20/20 hindsight of looking back many years later, I don't see it that way anymore. When I consider what that time was about and what it did for me, I no longer think it was just nice. I think it was necessary.

The Necessity of Learning What You Want

I couldn't put it into words then, but I was practicing knowing what I want. I exercised this with more intention and dedication in those forty days than I had for perhaps the forty years that came before that. I think I missed the significance of it because I didn't know it was a thing a person could *need* to practice. But it was. And I did.

I learned to pay attention to sparks of desire in the face of all the other important and urgent things clamoring for my time and attention. I practiced holding space for my desires rather than pushing them away or silencing them or dismissing them. I engaged with my wants with acceptance rather than harshness and judgment. Looking back now, I can see that it was a kind of rehearsal—making room to notice, directing my awareness toward what I wanted, linking that desire to action, and repeating it all again the next day. I didn't have words yet to articulate why this was important, but I was building the habit of honoring my desires rather than shutting them down. Through simple repetition, I learned that knowing what you really want is not only worth practicing but necessary for living a life that is more alive, authentic, and abundant.

Perhaps most significantly, the forty-day experiment gave me a new friendship with my desires. I became reacquainted with a part of myself that I had lost touch with. What began as an idea to help me recover from the pain of rejection restored my relationship with my desires, forever shifting how I would see them from that point forward.

Imagine going out to lunch with a friend, and she leans over her menu to tell you something she's excited about. Her voice is eager, and she wants to know if you'd be a part of her plans too. But you don't want to listen to her, and you don't do anything to hide your annoyance. In fact, you tell her that she's superficial and criticize her for not caring about things you deem more significant. Whenever she offers suggestions to address the concerns you have, you tell her she must be on another planet because her ideas would never work. Whenever your friend tries to speak, you cut her off. When she does manage to get a word in, you belittle her, diminish her perspective, and tell her that she doesn't have anything to offer. You communicate that you think of her as selfish and untrustworthy. Imagine that this isn't just the dynamic for a couple of hours at lunch but for every interaction between you. Over time, what kind of relationship would you expect to have?

It's terrible to think of speaking to anybody you care about this way. It sounds awful, as it should. But what many people don't realize is that this is only a slight exaggeration of how a lot of us relate to our desires. We don't treat our desires the way we would treat a friend we care for. When this becomes an ingrained pattern, it erodes the relationship we have with this part of ourselves. The sad part is that we're worse off for it. Desires intended to be life-giving are lost to us, and their wisdom becomes inaccessible.

I'd nearly missed the point of the experiment. The repeated action of doing what I wanted every day for forty days, like learning a new recipe or moving my desk from one side of the room to the other, was never about external things, like success or doing something impressive. It was about becoming friends with my desires. Isn't this how we build relationships that matter, anyway? From within the everyday space of simple shared experiences, slowly repeated over time. Practicing listening to my desires recovered a quality of relationship with a part of myself that I had lost somewhere between making mud cookies and becoming an adult.

The experiment wasn't as simple as it had seemed at the time. Above all else, the value of it was relational rather than productive.

Experimenting with listening to this part of myself day after day allowed me to relate to my desires with openness and trust, replacing distance and silencing. The gift of those forty days was learning how to befriend my desires. And, like my actual human friendships, it's a relationship that has added so much to my life.

I still think about those early days of investigating the realm of knowing what I want. I think about how whatever the opposite of an out-of-body experience is called, that's what it was. It was like coming home to myself. I felt rooted and certain. Those days taught me how to know what I want. Not because any other person or thing told me what my desires should be. I knew what my desires were because my life, my being, and my body told me. I believe this embodied, holistic discovery of desires is one of the most sacred ways anybody can ever uncover the truth about what they truly want.

Knowing What You Want

Knowing what you want is a process, a relationship, and an embodied discovery of what it means for you to thrive. When you know what you want, it lights a path toward aliveness and walks you through it. It helps you see who you have been made to be and then guides you to take the steps to become that person. It will remind you time and time again not to fracture yourself to fit in someone else's boxes, that the world is bigger than you give it credit for, and that there's room for what you have to bring to it. It will speak to you about abundance. It will teach you how to believe in yourself, maybe more fully than ever before. You will heal slowly and surely. And it will show you how to explore, dream, and learn to trust yourself. When you know what you want, you learn how to create a grounded life, one that is imperfect but that you're absolutely in love with.

I chose the title, *The Magic of Knowing What You Want*, to honor this knowing and invite you to experience it too. This knowing forges new, healing ways of relating to ourselves and the world. It helps us unlearn messages from a society that would teach us to distrust ourselves, stay small, and forget our power. It shows us that our deepest desires are closer than we think and how to discover them. This knowing exists to help us become more whole. It changes us, and it's magical when we learn how to be present to it.

I believe that if more of us learn how to do this, we will unlock so much good, not only in our own lives but also in the lives of the people and communities we care about most. This matters because our world is precious and it's a mess, with daily headlines full of fresh ways to break our hearts. It's no surprise to anyone that we need new ways of thriving that will enact real solutions, systemic change, and collective ways forward. I can't help but ask—what if our desires can be a wise guide to get us there? Our desires have something important to say. They can shake things up in profoundly generative ways to help us create what the world needs. The more I work with people coming alive to who they are, the stronger my hunch is that our desires have a central role to play in us, and the world is waiting to welcome the beautiful work our desires are capable of.

Overview

Truly knowing what you want requires both thought and practice, and we'll explore the balance of those essentials throughout this book. In chapter 1, we'll discuss desire fog, the condition of being confused about your desires, and how common it can be. In chapter 2, we'll talk about the interconnectedness of purpose and desire and rewrite the limited narratives that tell us desires are selfish or frivolous. In chapter 3, we will engage with the four types of questions that tend to drown out our desires as well as what to ask instead, so that we can begin to identify what might be blocking us from listening well to our desires. Beginning in chapter 4, we'll discuss the four-stage pathway to knowing your desires and living them out, called the authentic alignment pathway. Each stage focuses on one primary question and how to engage with it. Chapter 4 will cover the first stage, calibration, and the importance of paying attention to how you come alive. Chapter 5 will cover the second stage, expansion, and explore our relationship to limits and possibilities. Chapter 6 will discuss the third stage, experimentation, and how to use an experimental approach to create clarity around your desires. Chapter 7 will cover the fourth and final stage, integration, and what it looks like to interpret and respond to outcomes in the process of bringing our desires to life. Next, in chapter 8, we'll move to the idea of desire-based goal setting and how it differs from traditional forms of goal setting. And finally, in chapter 9, we'll end with what it means to look for the mystery and magic in our own stories.

By design, each chapter offers a learning component or a reflection prompt. The authentic alignment pathway was developed from thousands of real-life stories. The principles, ideas, and tools in this book were formed within the context of conversations and dialogue with real people through my work as a coach and consultant, and I didn't want to leave that out. Plus, I have to ask how all this fits in your life since no one is more of an expert on you than, well, you. These reflection prompts are designed to draw out your experiences and the wisdom already embedded in your life. They're not an afterthought. They're kind of the main dish. We will explore the overall principles of this process, and I'll also share stories and examples, but I ultimately want you to walk away feeling equipped to make meaningful connections in your life.

If I had it my way, I'd love to sit across from you with a cup of coffee, ask you these questions, and talk deeply about you and your life because I believe this is where the good stuff happens. Since we can't have this kind of chat, the least I can do is give you the prompts and questions I'm dying to ask you. I've designed this to be simple since I know you're probably busy, even if, like me, you're trying to work on how to slow down. Each prompt is designed to take only twenty to thirty minutes but gives you a strong return on investment. You're welcome to spend more time if you want, but it's more important to find what works for you and feels doable.

Because of this emphasis on conversation and relationships, I recommend going through this process with others. As always, listen to yourself, but if you're up for it, I think you'll find it valuable to dialogue with someone else. This could mean starting a discussion-based small group like a book club, which allows you to learn from listening to others' stories as well as reflecting on your own. If a group setting isn't right for you, you could talk about this one-on-one with a good friend, partner, coach, therapist, or mentor. Personal growth isn't solely an individual endeavor, and supportive relationships are an invaluable ingredient. I can point to many crucial inflection points in my journey where the trusted people in my life helped me notice essential insights I would surely have missed on my own. I can't imagine my process without them and their ability to hold space for me. When we show up for one another, it's life-changing, so if you can find a way to receive the gift of going through this process with someone else, it will serve you well.

As we begin, it's also important to acknowledge that being able to consider one's desires is a privilege. People in survival mode often don't have the capacity to think about what they want. People who struggle with chronic illness tell me their only desire is to be healthy or free of pain. Disabled folks talk about their desire to live within a society that sees them and cares for their needs. I have found it important to recognize my privilege as someone whose life circumstances and resources permit me not to be in survival mode, and how this position of privilege allows me to engage with my desires in a way that not everybody has. I know this journey isn't one that everyone gets to go on as much as I wish they could, and I need to be thoughtful about this. So, as we get started, I also want to acknowledge this aspect of the kind of work we're doing.

Start Small

Nowadays, I wonder what would've happened if I'd never gone to the beach. What would be different if I had never set out to spend forty days figuring out what honoring my desires felt like? Would I have learned to notice the bigger desires that were to come later? Would I have been able to walk away from situations that weren't right for me? Would I ever have discovered how liberating my desires could be? Of course, it's impossible to know for sure, and questions like these are unanswerable, but I strongly suspect that I wouldn't have been able to notice and act on any of the bigger, riskier desires to come without practicing over and over with the small ones first. I never could have guessed that something as small as going to the beach could mean learning how to get myself free.

So, if you're starting with something that feels rather small, remember there is magic in small things. Keep in mind that it can be the smallest sparks that create the most meaningful changes in your life, work, and leadership. I have never gotten over the thrill of witnessing others create thriving in the big or small ways that matter most to them. When I watch it happen with the people I get to work with, I beam and cheer and celebrate with my whole heart. I love to see it and can't wait to see it in you.

PART 1

The WISDOM of OUR DESIRES

1

What Do You Really Want?

Writers usually begin a book with an idea or a story to share. I come with a question.

What do you really want?

It's an age-old question but one that we may never outgrow. Inner and outer transitions can cause this question to come back repeatedly, even if a past version of you had it all figured out. It's a big question, but one that affects the very smallest elements of our lives. It's a question that's everywhere, but we aren't taught where to go to find answers for it. Based on hundreds of conversations I've had with others, as well as my own story, "What do you really want?" is only a simple question until you try to answer it meaningfully.

When I set out to put my coaching certification into practice, I was eager to get started. It sounded exciting to help people use knowledge of their strengths, assessment results, and newfound self-awareness to accomplish what they wanted most. There was only one small problem.

They didn't actually know what they wanted.

Conversations often went like this:

Me: Here's your profile and what it means.

Them: Wow, this makes so much sense, but now what? What do I do with this insight?

Me: This is how you work, but where to go with it depends on what you want. So, let me ask you—what do you want?

Time and time again, I kept getting the same responses.

"I don't ask myself what I want."

"I can't remember the last time someone asked me that, and I don't know."

"Not only do I have no idea what I really want but I have no clue how to figure it out."

My training hadn't prepared me for this. Responses like these challenged my preconceived notions of what coaching would entail. Because I didn't see it coming, I didn't know what to make of it at first. As someone who had experienced my own fair share of confusion about what I wanted, it's ironic I wasn't aware that other people go through the same thing. But as this pattern continued, I heard more and more real-life examples of a phenomenon nobody seemed to be talking about, and I wanted to know more. I couldn't ignore the pain, confusion, and angst it caused in people's lives to feel like they had nothing to say about an essential question we're all supposed to answer instinctively.

Shouldn't it be *easy* to know what you want? Isn't it as natural and unconscious as breathing? Listening to people's stories has shown me that our desires aren't always plain to decipher. There's a lot more to them, and sometimes we need help to uncover and understand them. These stories are a lot like mine, and they might be a lot like yours too. Our desires can be challenging, and not discussing this reality makes it much worse.

These repeated conversations showed me how the simple question of what you want can go from straightforward to complex *fast*. When you are lost about how to answer, that confusion feels like a crushing wave of emotions. I call this desire fog, and it is frustrating, stress-inducing, and tricky to navigate.

Desire Fog

People told me they'd lived with desire fog for weeks, months, or years. These same people were often clear about what others—their bosses, parents, organizations, or partners, just to name a few—wanted for them, but when it came to what they themselves wanted, they were at a loss. The word "should" came up often, as it seemed easier to name obligation and expectation than sincere desire. People carried assumptions about what they "ought" to want, but they were not always able to tell where those beliefs came from, or whether that thinking was serving them.

Of course, this wasn't everyone. Naturally, some people knew what they wanted personally and professionally. People told me about dreams they had, like making significant career changes, investing in their growth and wellness, starting businesses, going back to school, cultivating warm and loving friendships and families, pursuing adventures, and repairing important relationships in their lives. For people who knew what they wanted, I could coach them to work on ideas, goals, and next steps to realize their desires, and the coaching process provided relational support for taking a dream from desire to reality.

But for those who struggled to articulate their desires in the first place, I might as well have been asking them to take a final exam for a class they'd never attended. Having access to endless options and possibilities didn't feel exciting; it felt overwhelming because there was nothing to help them edit, curate, or sort those opportunities. It's hard to create alignment when you don't know what you're trying to align with. What's the right next step when you have no idea what you want and can't remember the last time you asked yourself that question? It turns out it's hard to say, and many people never learn how to navigate any of these confusing realities.

To put it another way, most people are never taught how to want.

It's not because people with desire fog lack capability or capacity. In my experience, they are kind, talented, brilliant human beings. They possess character and care deeply about others. They want to make a positive difference in the lives of their families, loved ones, organizations, and communities. They care about goodness, justice, and the world, and they want to leave things better for the next generation. They are accomplished and have degrees, roles, and life experiences that reflect their considerable strengths and achievements. They can usually tell you what they *could do*. It's just that *could do* can be a very far cry from *want to do*.

What Desire Fog Sounds Like

In these conversations, I hear sadness. Many people tell me how they feel alone and isolated, as if they are the only person in the world without a compelling answer for what they want out of life. Many of them express significant amounts of embarrassment, guilt, or shame. As if the agony of desire fog wasn't enough, it also seems to come with quite a bit of self-judgment.

Here are a few snapshots of these conversations.

Mina came to me when she was on the cusp of a big transition. She was leaving the job and organization she'd been a part of for more than eight years, and she had a lot of clarity about why that was necessary. But Mina did not know what was supposed to come next. We sat across from each other one afternoon at a café, and when I asked her what she might want moving forward, she confessed she was at a loss.

"I sort of know what I *don't* want, but if you ask me what I do want, I honestly don't know. When I think about the future, I can't picture anything. I feel like I'm trying to pull something out of thin air. The things I think of make me second-guess myself, and I immediately have so many more questions. It feels confusing, and I'm overwhelmed."

To Mina, "What do you want?" was a daunting question. She was afraid that not knowing what she wanted in this chapter of her life meant that it might be unknowable. When you're struggling to gain clarity about your desires, it's easy to feel like your confusion might never end.

Ivy called me to ask about working together, and when we met, she told me about how she had never been good at articulating her desires. She'd spent most of her life seeking to please others but was noticing the enormous toll that was taking on her, mentally, emotionally, and spiritually. She desperately wanted to have a clear idea of what she wanted but didn't know where to start. When I told her how many of the people I work with felt exactly like she did, she exclaimed, "Oh my goodness, that is such a relief. I thought I was the only one that struggled with this. You're telling me that other people do too?"

To Ivy, "What do you want?" was a lonely question. She was convinced that everyone else had it all figured out, and she was the only person in the world who didn't know what to make of their desires. Believing that feels terrible because if everyone else can do it, what's wrong with you? People tell me they don't talk about their experience with desire fog with the people they're close to because they're embarrassed to admit they don't know what they want. And I get it. When society prizes achievement, ambition, and going after what you want, it can feel like a personal failure if you're struggling to name your desires to begin with. It can feel so isolating.

When Stephanie came to me, she was starting to come up for air after a challenging season. She was in the final stages of closing down the nonprofit organization she had founded. Starting this organization had been her dream; deep down, she'd believed it would be what she would do for the rest of her life. But as she experienced burnout, she had to admit that it was time to step away from "her baby."

When you watch a dream flicker out, discerning what you want next is complicated because you never expected to need to figure it out again. It can feel like "going backward." When that's the case, "What do you want?" reminds you that you are unexpectedly starting again, which comes with its own grief.

If any of these stories resonate with you, simply asking what you want probably won't get you any closer to meaningful answers. Well-intentioned but simplistic advice like "find your passion and follow your heart" isn't likely to do too much either. Telling Mina, Ivy, Stephanie, or any of the people I've worked with to just figure it out doesn't help, and assuming that's the only starting point is alienating. I call this *pull-up advice* because it reminds me of the online tutorial that told me that the way to do a pull-up—as someone who has never been able to do one in their entire life—is to "put your hands on the bar and pull your chin up over the top of it." You don't say? Gee, thanks.

Desire fog is real. When you're in it, you need to know where to start. You need to shrink the looming questions down to small, doable steps. You need a process that allows for organic and meaningful insight. You need new ways of thinking (principles, thought patterns, and paradigms that will help you frame the process) and doing (intentional practices, action steps, and handholds that ground your journey in the reality of your life). You need to know that clarity is closer than you think, and you can become someone who can create powerful insight, alignment, and momentum with your true desires.

You, too, can learn how to want.

Learning How to Want

Most of us have not been taught how to pay attention to the most important things that help us have a good relationship with our desires. There are reasons why desire fog happens, and we'll explore what they are together. If this is something you struggle with, you're not alone. There are so many other people who are on a journey to find their way toward clarity and alignment with their desires. Many of them have experienced the same questions, feelings, hopes, and fears that you may be holding too. Together, I hope we can spark more honest conversations about this area of our lives and how to navigate it well.

It may sound strange to say, but knowing what you want is something that you can get better at. It's a skill set you can improve, like learning to play a beautiful song on the guitar or creating great homemade dumplings. If you've never had any guitar lessons and someone handed you a guitar and told you to play your favorite song, that wouldn't go very well. But if that person taught you some basic chords and gave you some beginning steps, you would get better with practice. Growing up, I used to marvel at how my dad could use a rolling pin to transform flour and water into perfect dumpling skin circles while my mom mixed the tasty ingredients to fill them, resulting in what I considered the best meal ever. When I asked how they were able to perform this magic, usually while lamenting my own misshapen attempts to help, they'd always say the same thing: "It's because we've practiced." It's the same with navigating your desires. When this area feels tricky, sometimes it's because we haven't learned how to do it yet.

The pathway we'll use to figure out what we want is called the authentic alignment pathway. It gives you the tools and practices you'll need to grow this essential skill set. As I have worked through this pathway with people, I've heard their questions and confusion. But I have also had the honor of witnessing how it doesn't stop there. I have seen how the large questions become more bite-sized and doable through simple categories and actions. I've observed what it looks like to gain personal, meaningful, and embodied clarity. I know it's possible for you because I've seen it.

If you're someone who is already good at knowing what you want, that's great too. Sometimes people tell me that learning this pathway helps them identify and affirm the things they've been doing intuitively. If that's you, I hope this enables you to understand more about what's working for you, why that's the case, and how to keep going with even more intentionality. The pathway can highlight the things you're doing already that are working well for you so you can amplify them. I'm a big believer in noticing bright spots and leaning into them.

Mina, Ivy, Stephanie, me, and you, we're part of a fascinating, ongoing conversation with ourselves, each other, and the divine about what it means to form a relationship with our desires—some of us maybe for the first time. The relationship you have with your desires can be one of your life's most important and liberating relationships. If you long for that, I'm here to tell you that you're on the right track.

I can't take all the angst out of the question "What do you really want?" But together, we'll examine some of our assumptions about desires, work toward clarity and alignment, and weave together who we are with what we want to create a life of thriving. Desire fog can be frustrating, but it doesn't have to be where your story ends.

Surprising and Inevitable

When you discover your deep desires, it's really something. The best way I can describe it comes from a podcast I listen to in my regular rotation, NPR's *Pop Culture Happy Hour*, which, if you didn't already know, is perfect for those stuck-in-traffic afternoons when you want something engaging, not overly serious, but still enlightening. In one particular episode, the topic of the day was the all-time best series finales in TV history.

Before each member of the panel shared their picks (*The Americans*, *The Bob Newhart Show*, *Veep*, and *The Good Place*, in case you were curious), they spent some time discussing the criteria they used to make their choices. One of the hosts, Glen Weldon, described the rubric he utilizes: "Turns out there's a formula for narrative satisfaction that is *surprising* plus *inevitable* equals *satisfying*. It might sound like they're at cross-purposes, but they really aren't because surprising means, in the moment, you didn't see it coming. Inevitable because the second you step away . . . and you reflect, you go, 'Oh, they've been building to this; they've laid the track, and they've honored the work that they've put in, but I could never have guessed it.'"[1]

This exciting combination of surprising and inevitable is what I see happen for people when they venture toward knowing what they really want. Surprise happens when you discover desires that you hadn't realized were there and that maybe you thought were lost a long time ago. Or you discover desires that feel beyond what you've let yourself dare to want. Surprising moments take place when the right opportunity comes knocking at just the right time, even though you may never have seen it coming. It surprises you because it's so much better than what your fears told you to settle for.

Inevitable happens when you step back and see the clues that were there all along. You encounter something that feels like it was always meant to be, like a puzzle piece finding its intended spot. You get to the inevitable when you look back on your own story and see the track that was laid before you could understand what you were seeing. You discover a picture of goodness that feels custom-made for you. You wonder how you didn't see it there all along.

Surprising and inevitable—the markers of a well-written narrative that are even better as a well-lived story.

I see this all the time. I saw it when Max accepted a new role that was a perfect mix of challenge and support. I saw it when April's childhood love of saving and splicing video clips led to a successful career in video editing. I saw it when Sarah's experience living abroad confirmed a passion for doing international organizational development. I saw it when Rebekah decided to continue to invest in teaching watercolor workshops, a fitting blend of her experience as an artist and a therapist. I saw it when Stephanie told me she was on the brink of launching a business designing and planting native gardens. I saw it when Evelyn made a significant career move to work in philanthropy, which she'd dreamed of but feared would be too hard to break into. I saw it when Isabelle told me she'd successfully changed career paths and started as a DEI director in higher education. I saw it when Kate told me she'd gotten a job at a leading research lab, integrating her expertise as an engineer with her passion for birding and conservation. I saw it when Bora was chosen by Reese Witherspoon's book club to be one of five literary mentees for the novel she'd been writing for years. The beautiful, moving blend of surprising and inevitable isn't just for the characters we watch on our favorite TV shows. It can be for us. If you want it, it can be for you too.

Magic unfolds when you discover how your desires are speaking to you to create clarity in your life. You learn what you were made to do. You find the specific, unique hues that are your soul's perfect shade of thriving. You respond to the question of what you really want because you know exactly what it feels like in your body, and your life has shown you the answers. When you know what you want, it changes you. It'll make you gasp in surprise, and it will also make you say, "Of course. It was there all along." A little surprising. Inevitable in hindsight. Deeply satisfying. I can't think of anything better for you and the beautiful story your life is writing.

{ REFLECTION PROMPT }

Noticing Desire Fog

Take a moment to settle into a calm, relaxed state. You can stretch, roll your shoulders, or take a few deep breaths to settle down. This reflection is a chance to connect with your current experience with desire fog.

1. At this time, how does desire fog show up in your life? Is this similar to or different from what you've experienced in the past?
2. Who are the people in your life that can help you process where you're at and what you're learning?
3. What are the hopes you have for your process? What kind of clarity are you looking for?

Purpose and Desire

A Tale of Two Siblings

Purpose is well-liked and respected—his younger sister, Desire, not so much.

Purpose is often invited to important places by important people who don't look twice at Desire. When Purpose speaks, he's articulate, impressive, and confident, and everyone is always eager to listen to whatever he has to say. And why wouldn't they? He's such a star and everyone knows it. He's given countless keynote presentations, and there's no room he walks into where he isn't the VIP. It gets rather tricky to keep track of his calendar, but that's the price of being in demand. Oh, and did I mention the stacks of books he's written?

Desire, on the other hand, has a very different story.

Once, Desire tried to show up at the same crucial meeting as her brother, and it was so shocking that everybody lost focus. People were too polite to say anything out loud, but they were all thinking the same thing: "What's *she* doing here? How did she even get past security?"

In their defense, it's true that Desire can be a little wild. For starters, she's got a bad habit of asking unnerving questions at the wrong time, and she's practically allergic to doing something simply because "it's the way it has always been done." If I didn't know better, I'd say that she doesn't really care about rules at all and prefers to live with nuance, intuition, and mystery over black-and-white thinking. Unlike Purpose, she didn't go to a fancy school, doesn't have the right credentials, and doesn't speak the same lingo as everyone else. This makes it hard to take her ideas seriously at times. It's not surprising that after years of this, she's become known by the same all-too-familiar labels—too out-there, too selfish, too frivolous, too much.

Serious people pay attention to Purpose, but they don't listen to Desire. Whatever would be the point?

But lately, Desire is starting to wonder about the way things have always been. Is it possible that she's been underestimated and written off too soon? Is there a chance that her point of view is something people need after all, and her questions are worth more time and attention than anybody thought? She's beginning to think that she has more to say and that there's more for her to do. With our world so desperate for healing and transformation, maybe the individuals and communities who can make a difference in the tangle of crisis and opportunity are precisely the kinds that need the power of *both* Purpose and Desire in their lives.

Could it be that Purpose and Desire are actually meant to be collaborators in the process of discovering our thriving? Is it possible that they were never intended to exist in separate silos? Working together, perhaps they can lead us to a deeper discovery of flourishing and joy-filled impact. What if the good we're looking for comes from the mutual, generative partnership of Purpose and Desire?

Suspicion and Desire

I remember a conversation in which I told someone I was scheduled to speak at an upcoming event to a group of women on the topic of desires. Without knowing anything about what I planned to say, the person immediately responded with a look of concern and said, "Well, not all desires are good, so you have to be careful." Fascinating response.

Of course, they had a point, and, in fact, not all desires are good, but the instant suspicion of the very concept of desires stood out to me because we don't typically do this with other things in life, even if they are a mixed bag in reality. Before I had children, not once did anybody tell me that not all kids grow up to be good people and that I should be cautious. Even if that's technically true, it would be a really strange thing to tell someone. To say I was speaking on the topic of desires was as if I had announced that I planned to get up on stage and hand out hall passes for the worst of human nature. I imagined that if, instead, I had stated I was speaking about purpose, they wouldn't have given it a second thought, and they would have been happy to offer their unequivocal, enthusiastic support. It seemed to me that the idea of desire sets off instant alarm bells that the topic of purpose never does.

This dynamic highlights a pervasive belief about the role of desires in our lives. In chapter 1, we talked about how hard it can be to know what we really want. We challenged the assumptions that everyone automatically knows their desires and that questions about our true desires should be easy ones to answer, and discussed how prevalent desire fog can be. In this chapter, we will look at a different but equally common assumption that says all desires are suspicious and portrays them in a largely negative light. This perspective makes it harder to know how to relate to our desires in a healthy way.

I find that most personal development spaces are built on the assumptions that either everyone knows what they want implicitly *or* that being a good person means suppressing your desires in favor of focusing solely on other people. Purpose is seen as noble and, therefore, valid. Desires are not. In many cases, desire is painted as an enemy to living a life of meaning, rather than a potential ally. As I've read and listened to countless teachings about creating a life of purpose, the messages I hear repeatedly are:

What you want must be bad somehow.

Desires are selfish. Purpose is heroic.

Finding purpose comes from focusing on what other people want rather than what you want.

Building a good life means ignoring your desires.

Being a good person means disregarding your desires.

Nothing good comes from thinking about your own
desires.

Thinking about what you want is a sign of immaturity
or a lack of character.

While I see how sentiments like this are well-intentioned
and have their own reasoning, this school of thought does
not do justice to our desires and what they have to offer.
There's so much more nuance and wisdom to desires and
what they can be in our lives. The answer isn't as binary or
simplistic as painting all desires for all people as wholly negative without considering what could also be positive about
them. It's easier to treat desires as unconditionally negative,
but that doesn't mean it's right.

When I started to do a deeper dive into this tension, I
wrestled with my mixed feelings about desires, and I realized they were coming not only from external messages
like the conversation I had about the women's event but
also from internalized messages about the significance of
desires. When I did my forty-day experiment, nobody told
me that what I was doing was regressive, but I had a voice
in my head telling me that maybe it was. I remember feeling uneasy, not knowing how to reconcile feeling drawn
to think more about my desires with not wanting to be a
selfish person. Seeing this made me realize that negative
messages about desires weren't just "out there." It's always
disconcerting when you realize that the call is coming from
inside the house, and I sensed that it might be time to reexamine some of my perspectives because they didn't match
up with the good I saw unfolding in my life as I engaged
with my desires.

Old Narratives and Desire

I couldn't look at my thinking on this subject without also reexamining my experience of faith. In my life, those things were inseparably connected. My participation in church and proximity to evangelicalism played a central role in shaping my attitudes about my desires. When I started to question how religion impacted these narratives, there was a lot to unpack. I know that not everyone has had this experience, and someone else's religious background may or may not look like mine, so I'm not assuming this is everybody's story, but for me, my religious formation was vital to revisit, as I'd spent decades in this context. My faith is central and important to me, but I hadn't ever given much consideration to how its messages around desires made an impact on my life.

When you listen to what is taught about desires in the context of evangelicalism, the guilt-inducing message is usually that caring about your desires means caring too little about God.[1] If you were truly a godly person, you wouldn't think at all about what you want; you would only be concerned with God's will. This rhetoric sounds pious, but it raises a lot of questions: Who holds the power to define what the will of God is? Who benefits from presenting your desires and God's will as an either/or binary? If I've been highly committed to my faith for more than twenty years of my life, yet the message is that what I want is categorically selfish and needs to be suppressed, doesn't that seem inconsistent with a worldview that says we are created in the image of the divine, and God wants to draw near to us in our humanity? Isn't something off if my core understanding of self is supposed to be that I'm a worthless worm of a human who can't possibly be trusted to know what she wants?

I considered how patriarchy plays a role in this because, in many evangelical contexts, men's desires are often called visionary, while women's desires are not given such a generous interpretation. I came to suspect that saying you uphold God's will above your wicked desires makes for a snappy sound bite on Sunday morning, but without consideration of a diverse set of lived experiences, it can be used to perpetuate a damaging brand of people-pleasing and unquestioning obedience to hierarchical leadership that lacks the nuance needed to navigate our lives, ultimately causing people to abdicate the dignity and agency given to us as human beings created in God's image. I also started to interrogate who benefits when people who have been historically marginalized and underrepresented, such as women, people of color, disabled people, or LGBTQIA+ folks, are told that they don't get to ask for what they want.

Instead of doubling down on a way of thinking that began to sound a lot like a form of self-erasure, I learned about mystics like Teresa of Avila, who taught that one's journey of faith was like a series of rooms in a castle that evolves with maturity over time.[2] I felt invited into a growing, evolving experience of faith that wasn't rigid and controlling. Under the leadership of womanist theologians, I heard a call to reclaim oneself, one's body, and one's full being in a way that didn't have the harsh lines between secular and sacred I was used to hearing about.[3] *Womanism* is a term coined by author and scholar Alice Walker to describe a perspective that centers the experiences, viewpoints, and liberation of Black women.[4] Womanist scholars modeled the deep importance of seeing things from an intersectional lens. I learned about the core values of restorative justice, the first one of which says that the true self in everyone is good, wise, and powerful.[5] I found this to be a refreshing counter to the narrative that humans are solely and forever depraved. I studied Ignatian spirituality, which teaches that desires in a spiritually integrated person are essential to growth and are an indispensable way to hear the voice of God.[6] I learned from Native American teachers pointing to an Indigenous worldview rooted in the interconnectedness of all things rather than binaries.[7] They offered a holistic understanding of ourselves in relation to Creator and creation that felt both freeing and compelling. And I returned to Jesus himself, who is introduced as the Word made flesh, the embodiment of the cosmos, whose very first words recorded in the book of John are, "What do you want?" (John 1:38).

Selfishness and Desire

Of course, individualistic self-focus and selfishness are problems in our world. That's not a difficult case to prove, given the degree of evil and harm that surrounds us on a far too regular basis. This cannot be ignored. If you're a terrible person who does evil with no remorse toward your fellow human beings, you're not someone who should be told to pay more attention to your desires. But I've also come to recognize that discernment would say that just because something is *a* problem doesn't mean it is the *sole* problem, which also means it may not be *our only* problem.

Being selfishly focused on your desires isn't the only way that desires can be unhealthy. Aristotle argued that moral

44

behavior is the mean between the two extremes of excess and deficiency. Too much courage, and you're prone to foolish behavior. Too little, and you're unable to take action when needed.[8] To be sure, an excess of desire without consideration of communal needs leads to selfishness, entitlement, and harm. Yet a deficiency of desire leads to toxic passivity and self-erasure, preventing the creation of flourishing in our lives. This also damages the collective good.

You don't walk into the pharmacy and start taking any random person's prescription. In the same way, when you hear teaching about desires, you need to ask yourself—whose prescription is this? It belongs to someone, but is it yours? Some people need to be told to think less about what they want and more about what others desire in order to move toward true thriving. But that group of people isn't the same as many of the people I've talked to who tell me that their struggles are rooted in pleasing people, a lack of healthy boundaries, being underestimated and silenced, and over-functioning for the sake of others. I've learned that for the latter, advice to ignore desires or see them only as a force of harm to be suppressed may be akin to handing them someone else's prescription.

Desires don't have to be a license for individualistic selfishness. Our desires can be important without being only about us. Done well, desires help us thrive, and as we listen to them, they help us contribute to the thriving of others. We don't have to subscribe to an unnecessary binary that pits purpose against desire, when the reality is that they dwell together and live within the same family. They are meant to be linked, and at their best, they work toward the same end—helping us build lives of joy, thriving, and impact.

Purpose and Desire

Purpose, as we know, is essential for creating a meaningful life. Desire without purpose easily becomes self-focused, but purpose also needs desire. This is because purpose without desire often leads to what we think we *should* do rather than a knowing of what we're *meant* to do.

To leave desire behind, even in search of something as significant as purpose, can point us to the grand, the grandiose, and the abstract rather than the grounded reality of our actual lives with everything human, limited, and magical about who we really are. When we do this, it leaves us with a top-down approach to crafting a life that happens by naming a directive about where we should go rather than by listening to who we really are and what our lives are actually saying. People tell me how approaching purpose as a directive makes it feel like an ideal so lofty that it feels inaccessible and unattainable. In my experience, purpose has shown itself to be a wonderful destination but a not-so-great starting point. When I felt at my most lost, if I had waited for clarity of purpose before moving forward, I'd still be waiting. This is why I'm so passionate about understanding how our desires have a crucial role to play in the discovery of what we were made to do.

Educator and author Parker Palmer describes it this way when he says, "Before I can tell my life what I want to do with it, I must listen to my life telling me who I am. I must listen for the truth and values at the heart of my own identity, not the standards by which I *must* live—but the standards by which I cannot help but live if I am living my own life."[9] When we bypass our true desires, we are at risk of crafting a life that looks great on paper but is disconnected from who we truly are and our personal best way of making a difference in the world. Burnout, misalignment, and languishing often follow, and the world misses out on some of the magic that we were meant to bring to it.

Our deepest desires are unwilling to accept a version of purpose, however noble, that isn't aligned with who we are. They will not allow us to follow an abstraction that is untethered from how our souls thrive. Our desires don't let us get away with not showing up as who we truly are. Desires require us to pay attention to our lived experiences in a way that purpose doesn't always ask us to do.

Your desires contain wisdom that doesn't reside anywhere else in your soul. Maybe it's possible to try to create a life of thriving where you're alienated from, distrustful of, and unable to engage with your desires meaningfully, but that's a harder road. No amount of hustle will let you outrun the truth of yourself.

Harsh separation of purpose and desire is often well-meaning but woefully shortsighted. Desires are direction, momentum, and discovery. Knowing your desires is just another way to say that you're being guided toward becoming the kind of person that you want to be. They are wise in uncovering the quality of thriving that is authentic to your true self. They help you build a life from the difference your flourishing makes. This is what it means to live with purpose and desire.

Purpose as Alignment

Integrating purpose and desire to create meaning in our lives often feels counterintuitive. It requires us to pay attention to small sparks of organic interest and desire, trusting that those glimmers will show us how they're connected to a greater purpose over time. But this can be unnerving because we're used to being told that a clear, strong sense of purpose always comes first, and we should have a "good reason" for everything we want. It's easy to feel unsettled when you're trying to live in the mystery of the way desire leads to a sense of purpose over time.

We won't always have the luxury of knowing what our desires will build in our lives before they show up. But, if we believe that desire and purpose are interconnected, we can trust that our desires create clarity of purpose. This is not as accepted as sitting down to write a beautiful and eloquent life purpose statement, but it is organic, grounded, and also valid. If you believe that listening to your desires generates alignment with what purpose is supposed to look like in your life, you'll be willing to trust the wisdom of your desires, even if you need a bit more patience to see how it comes together.

When we view purpose as a process of organic, holistic alignment, we recognize the roles of purpose and desire as partners and accomplices. Our desires provide small, organic moments of wisdom that slowly coalesce into greater meaning. The thriving born from this kind of partnership is expansive enough to care for the world and tangible enough to show us how to live that out, and it happens when we believe that what we want blazes a path to becoming who we were meant to be. Purpose and desire align because they were always supposed to work together.

What you truly want, as confusing as it may or may not seem at this moment, matters, and it matters for both you and the world. When you understand that purpose and desire are linked, your love for others should make you more, not less, interested in how your desires are speaking to you because you know that they lead you to discover a meeting of joy and meaning, an integration of impact and alignment, and a convergence of doing good and thriving. This is where our desires shine and what they were made to help us discover. I think the time is right to get serious about knowing what we want.

REFLECTION PROMPT

Desire Reality Check

We often hold inner tensions and paradoxes around our desires without even knowing it. When we dive deeper into our desires, we discover many things just under the surface, like the well-known graphic of an iceberg that depicts how little you truly see from above the surface of the water compared to what is underneath. This reflection exercise is designed to help you notice what might be happening under the surface in the unconscious assumptions, thoughts, and patterns that you carry about desires, so you can be more aware of those things. This helps set you up to be better able to navigate those dynamics. To do this, under each part of the grid, write down a few thoughts, feelings, or reactions that come to mind.

DESIRE REALITY CHECK

How does silencing my desires serve me?	How does silencing my desires **not** serve me?

How does silencing my desires serve others?	How does silencing my desires **not** serve others?

QUESTIONS FOR REFLECTION

1. What does this exercise show you about the assumptions that you have about desires?

2. If you had to sum up your relationship with your desires, how would you describe it? Do you tend to see desires as positive, negative, or a mix of both? What contributes to your perspective?

3. Do you sense an invitation or a next step from this reflection? If so, what is it?

3

The Four Types of Questions That Get in the Way and What to Ask Instead

A few months after the VP rejection, I met Chris and set up an informational interview with him in an effort to figure out the small matter of my future. I'd met him recently and found out that he worked for a company I was interested in, and he was generously willing to grab a coffee to chat about his experience. We'd coordinated a meetup, and I remember exhaling after arriving on time despite some particularly bad LA traffic. As we sat down at a table on the patio, I mentally patted myself on the back for being functional enough to take a productive, albeit small, step toward what was next.

That's until he asked me a question. You can probably guess the one. "So, what do you want?" It was a perfectly rational question to ask in the kind of conversation we were having. But his query set off a panicked, internal mini-crisis I desperately hoped was not obvious. My mind was a tumble of thoughts as I struggled to form a decent answer. Thoughts that went a little something like: What *do* I want anyway? What kind of question is that? What does it matter what I *want*? I don't even know what's possible to begin with. What's the point of saying I want something that could never happen anyway? As a matter of fact—why doesn't he tell me what he sees as viable options for me, and I'll let him know which one of those I want? Of course, it makes perfect sense that someone I've known for only a few weeks is more qualified to tell me what's possible for my life than I am. Even if I did know what I wanted, could I really be honest with him? What if I say something, and he laughs in my face because he thinks I'm ridiculously unqualified? How does *anyone* know what they want anyway? Like, *know*. What if I say something, but I'm wrong? Then what?

Finally, for good measure, I sprinkled on a healthy dose of defensiveness—How dare he have the audacity to ask me something so frustrating? Who does he think he is?! (Chris, if you're reading this, I can see how this was entirely my issue, not yours.) To move our conversation to safer territory, I gave a generic answer and hoped that would be enough to back away from this Pandora's box for the time being. Later, when I returned to my car, I still didn't have a good answer to his question. I also wondered why on earth this simple, reasonable thing to ask had felt so loaded, and I thought, *Looks like I've got some big feelings about this.* Pretty perceptive, I know.

What happened to me during an everyday coffee appointment is what happens to a lot of us when we ask what we want. What begins as a straightforward question ends up stirring up an avalanche of other questions that come attached to challenging emotions like fear, shame, insecurity, and anxiety. Asking about your desires can be a vulnerable question to start with, but it gets even more fraught when it triggers so many other questions and feelings. This is why simply asking (or being asked) what you want doesn't always mean you can give a good answer.

This is human and understandable. When it comes to our desires, we ask a lot of questions because we often have valid concerns. We question what's feasible because it's not easy to know if our dreams are realistic. We ask questions about our qualifications because it's hard to gauge if we're being brave or delusional. It's confusing to make a big shift in our lives; if it were easy, we would have done it already. It's tricky to start new things, and it's human nature to struggle with the ups and downs of the unknown, especially when we have hard realities like financial considerations to weigh. Pretending that any of this is easy isn't helpful. Asking questions is to be expected, but that also doesn't mean we shouldn't also become more cognizant of the way the questions themselves can either help or hinder our ability to find clarity. When we thoughtfully engage with questions, we'll be in a much better place to approach the process.

Primary and Secondary Questions

To find a path through the questions, we need to learn how to be better question-askers, which starts with remembering that not all questions are equally helpful. Some types of questions are highly important and critical to ask. Other types of questions generate more desire fog, especially when asked too soon, and don't help us move forward at all. We can be left more confused than we were before we started. This is why it's important to understand how questions work in the process of clarifying our desires.

In other words, some questions belong in the driver's seat, and other questions make really bad drivers. Primary questions help us pay attention to ourselves, be open to possibilities, and learn the best ways for us to take steps forward. They help us answer the question of what we really want in personally meaningful ways, and they are important to prioritize. When we ask primary questions, it helps us create the mindset and practices for bringing our desires to life with more clarity and creativity. These questions help us lean into the parts of ourselves that bring our desires to light. Primary questions are the good drivers that we want to put in the driver's seat.

Secondary questions, on the other hand, make it harder for us to listen to our desires. Given the chance, they will drive us around in circles, waste every bit of fuel we have, and drop us off in the middle of nowhere—zero stars on Uber. We're not going to spend our one wild and precious life letting these questions do that to us.

Some secondary questions express valid concerns, while others really don't. Because of the nature (emotionally charged) and number (so darn many) of these questions, they can best be described as *loud*. The emotional volume of secondary questions makes it hard to hear anything else. They shout fears, anxieties, and insecurities at us. When this is what's in our heads, it's no wonder it's hard to hear our desires speak. Listening to your wants is hard enough as it is, but when these questions are in your face and preying on your worst-case scenarios, it feels impossible. If you're a parent who has ever tried to hold an adult conversation while the kids are screaming nearby, you get it. These questions shout at us while our desires merely whisper.

We'll discuss primary questions in depth later, but I want to start with secondary questions. Since secondary questions are often louder and take up more space in our minds, I've found that it's easier to engage with primary questions after first naming and addressing secondary questions. Like I said, we need to tell our secondary questions to hand over the keys and take a backseat.

Once, after I spoke on this topic, someone came up to me and said, "I've never realized how much secondary questions dominate my thinking all the time. I think about them constantly, so it's no wonder why I have such a hard time listening to what I want." This happens to so many of us when we haven't stopped to consider the types of questions we ask ourselves. Paying attention to secondary questions is an important first step in learning not to let them take over or drown out what your desires want to say.

Secondary questions fall into four categories: competency questions, pragmatic questions, capitalistic questions, and permission questions. There's some overlap between them, but they each have their own dynamics. We'll discuss one type of question at a time, including what that type sounds like, how it creates problems as you relate to your desires, and what to ask instead. Some people identify strongly with one type of question. Others can see all four in their lives.

For now, simply notice what's true for you. We'll talk about better questions to ask, but first, we'll learn how to lower the volume on these loud, secondary questions.

Competency Questions

Competency questions cause us to doubt what we're capable of and tend to make us feel like what we want is out of reach because we lack the gifts or talents to attain it. Even if we can name what we want, that peanut-sized desire is inextricably linked to an elephant-sized sense of self-doubt. "I don't ask myself if I want to do what I'm excited about because I'd never be qualified or good enough to get there in the first place." Knowing what we want is irrelevant because we lack the competency anyway, or so this thinking goes. Competency questions cause us to focus on how we will inevitably fall short of our deepest desires.

Competency questions sound like:

Do I have what it takes?

Am I really capable of this? If not, then I should settle for what is most feasible.

I'm not capable of this because I don't have x, y, or z qualities or credentials, right?

What do I lack in terms of experience, skills, or talents? Let's do a complete inventory!

Who are all the more experienced and better qualified people to do this?

Am I the very best in the world at this? If not, I shouldn't pursue it at all.

A significant problem with these questions is a faulty gauge error, which is another way to say that I'm betting you aren't very good at assessing your abilities. Have you ever had friends tell you that you're selling yourself short? That's a good clue that this might be you. Coaching people has taught me how astoundingly bad most people are at naming their abilities, strengths, gifts, and talents. If you're the exception to the rule, that's amazing, and keep up the good work. But I've learned that many of us are pretty lousy at accurately assessing ourselves.

You may not be able to do everything in the entire world, but I believe you can do so much more than what you give yourself credit for. If you can't hold a tune, I'm not saying you need to pretend that you'll become the next Beyoncé. You don't need to create a grandiose self-concept, but you do need to interrogate your competency questions and learn to hold them with a big grain of salt. Not only do they not help you listen to your desires very well but they are often flat-out wrong and based on flawed assumptions. They keep you preoccupied with what you lack and why you don't have what it takes, rather than with your strengths, potential, and ability to learn. Plus, can you name anything good that has come from putting yourself down, focusing on everything you lack, and devaluing your own talent and experience? Yeah, me neither. So, maybe it's time to have competency questions take a backseat.

Instead of competency questions, ask yourself aliveness questions.

One of the most foundational questions you can ask about your life is what makes you come alive. Asking questions about aliveness rather than competency helps you pay attention to what truly lights you up rather than why you'll fall short. If you've ever had an experience where someone asked you if you were interested in a potential opportunity, and your knee-jerk response was to think about all the skills and qualifications you lacked, this is a perfect example of when to ask aliveness questions instead of competency questions.

Aliveness shows up in our lives when we find the moments that make us feel like time stands still. They are full of flow, energy, and enjoyment. As I'm sure you've noticed, not all the ways we can spend our time are equal. Sixty minutes spent doing something that makes you feel alive is night and day from the same amount of time spent doing something you find torturous. Aliveness happens when you discover the energizing, satisfying, and "I can't wait to do that again" experiences in your life.

When you discover something that lights you up, it is a huge deal, whether or not it's something you'd ever put on a résumé. I wish we celebrated one another's aliveness, not just our accomplishments. I love it when there's a big milestone, moment, or award, but wouldn't it be great if we celebrated the rare and beautiful act of discovering a piece of our aliveness? I wish we said things like, "You found something that makes you feel alive and that's an incredible discovery. That's worth celebrating," so much more than we do.

If you're tempted to feel insecure about your perceived incompetence and lack of credentials, notice how great you feel when you're doing what makes you come alive. Pay attention to how much you enjoy doing what you want to do. Shift your focus from external sources of confidence, such as qualifications and validation from others, to an internal experience of confidence that comes from doing something that truly lights you up. Outward confirmations of your abilities are great, but they're no replacement for experiencing the life-giving things that spring from your aliveness. After you've established what brings you life, you can always ask what programs, skills, or other credentials you might want to add to support that. That's where competency questions can be helpful. You can learn a new set of skills that supports your aliveness, but it's hard to go the other way around to try to generate aliveness where it doesn't exist.

Remember that other people can gauge your competency, and they can tell you what they think about your performance from their external vantage point. But nobody else can tell you what makes you feel alive. You owe it to yourself to keep that at the top of your mind and to pay attention not just to the concerns of competency but also to aliveness. Remind yourself that you can always learn new skills, add to your experience, and build up your competencies, but finding the things that make you feel alive and that you truly enjoy doing is rare stuff.

Affirmations help put your focus on what will help you grow. In fact, research supports the practice of doing affirmations for one's psychological wellness, and there is scientific evidence to suggest that the ventromedial prefrontal cortex (the part of the brain related to how we process emotions and our self-concept) becomes highly active during affirmations.[1] Positive affirmations are also linked to decreased stress, increased well-being, and greater openness to changing your behavior. You can choose an affirmation that resonates with you or create your own.

11 Affirmations for Aliveness

- I can learn anything I need to know.
- Working out of my deep joy is powerful.
- I choose to be proud of myself.
- I bring unique strengths to the things that I do.
- I do not compare myself to others. My journey is my own.
- I have potential that is waiting to be activated.
- I choose kind words to speak to myself.
- I am growing.
- I trust my joy.
- I am grateful for what energizes and inspires me.
- I have everything I need to do what I'm meant to do.

Aliveness Questions

- What do you do that you truly enjoy?
- Which things that you already do would you describe as the most fun?
- What things seem to come most easily to you?
- What's something you do where you feel like you receive as much as you give, if not more?
- What's a compliment someone's given you about something you've done that means a lot to you?
- What makes you light up?
- What makes you lose track of time?
- What do you like to do regardless of whether anyone "makes" you do it?
- What do you seem to learn quickly or easily?
- When was the last time you did something and felt like you couldn't wait to do it again?
- What does aliveness mean to you?

Pragmatic Questions

Pragmatic questions are the practical concerns that tell us to focus on what is realistic above everything else. They are similar to competency questions because both types focus on whether a desire is realistic, but pragmatic questions are geared toward all the ways our desires are impractical rather than focusing primarily on our inadequacies.

Pragmatic questions love to point out the infinite ways an outcome may fall short of our dreams. Market trends, sweeping assumptions and generalizations of what is possible, case studies of others who may have tried and *gasp* failed, and other tough-to-argue, "irrefutable" facts work to convince you that what you want is just wishful thinking. Is that really possible? Is that realistic? Isn't that just a pipe dream? These questions bring in doubt, paint your desires as something that could never happen in a million years, and focus on the impracticality of what you want. The natural conclusion of this says, What's the point of knowing what you want when none of it will ever happen anyway?

These questions sound convincing and well-intentioned, almost as if they have our best interests at heart. It can seem like they're doing us a favor by not letting us get our hopes up for fear of disappointment. The underlying assumption is that it would be unbearable to admit you wanted something only to not have it happen. Pragmatic questions pose as well-meaning protective measures against being let down. We never stop to question whether there are worse things than being disappointed.

Pragmatic questions sound like:

Can this *really* happen? (This one barely qualifies as a
question because it's rhetorical and means, "No, this
can't happen.")

Will I just be disappointed if I go for this? And if so, it's
better not to try, right?

Isn't this unrealistic? Isn't this impractical?

Can I see every one of the steps it would take to have
this work out?

This happens for other people, but could it ever happen
for me?

Or the converse: Look at how this didn't work out for
others; what makes me think I'm any different?

When pragmatic questions are in the driver's seat, you may
see brief glimpses of your desires, but they usually don't last
long before they're crushed. Pragmatic questions move fast.
They pounce on any sparks of desire before they have had a
fighting chance of survival. No sooner do you see an inkling
of a desire than these questions crush it. You never need anybody to rain on your parade because you've already done it to
yourself. It's no wonder that when you ask yourself what you
truly want, you don't have anything meaningful to say. Those
desires are long gone, silenced by this kind of interrogation.
Pragmatic questions can also make you agonize and get stuck
in a holding pattern, locked in an endless loop of questions.

I'm all for being practical, but the problem with pragmatism is that it's not a good starting place. When your
desires are new and vulnerable, they can be suffocated by

pragmatism applied too quickly or too forcefully. In Patrick Lencioni's Working Genius framework, there's a category of genius related to being realistic and doing excellent planning and execution.[2] But this ability doesn't typically function well if we insert it too soon in the creative process, when it's important to hold space for ideas and possibilities.

If you're beginning to engage with a desire, it doesn't matter if it's realistic. It's more important to protect that desire and give it breathing room. It's incredibly tender and vulnerable to acknowledge or speak a desire out loud, especially when it feels uncertain. When I see someone do this, I know they need to celebrate and draw out that desire. They do not need somebody to begin a game of twenty questions about logistics, feasibility, and being realistic.

It takes so little to deem a desire unrealistic and to trash it accordingly. Sometimes it feels like our ability to crush our desires in the name of being practical can be triggered by the smallest thing. It's true that disappointment is painful, but it doesn't always have to be the mortal enemy we've made it out to be, and we'll talk about this a lot more in chapter 7. If you want to avoid the trap of pragmatism, don't let yourself become consumed with whether a desire is realistic, especially before you've given it a fair chance. This is especially true if a desire is new or feels extra vulnerable. Tell yourself that, for now, it simply matters that it is *real*. Let that be enough. Give your desires enough air to breathe so you can see how they will grow. Practicality can wait. There will be time for that later.

Instead of pragmatic questions, ask yourself imagination questions.

Asking questions about imagination gives your desires space beyond the limits of pragmatism. Imagination makes room for creativity and doesn't allow practicalities to rule everything. It loves poetry, creativity, and myths. My ancestors looked up at the moon, saw a beautiful archer's wife on its surface, and told stories about the betrayal that separated her from the love of her life. Our ancestors needed to focus on survival, but they also looked to the stars and saw warriors, lions, and goddesses peering back at them. They created beauty, color, music, and stories. In our world today, we have to be pragmatic, but we can't forget that imagination is also part of what it means to be human. Dreams are born when our desires get to dance with imagination.

One practice that can help you embrace imagination is play. We usually think of work and rest as opposites, but I don't believe that's completely true. It's too easy to think of rest as a means of making you more productive so you can work harder. As Tricia Hersey discusses in her book *Rest Is Resistance*, rest is a human need like food, water, or air; everyone deserves rest.[3] I believe the true opposite of work is play. Play leads you to engage with what you do out of sheer joy and delight. It's the best medicine for an over-functioning sense of pragmatism. In a to-do list world, play matters.

One way to begin a regular practice of play is by reflecting on what you used to do for fun as a kid. What do you remember doing as a child? When you were little and had a long summer day of nothing, what did you spend your time doing? How did you pass the time when no parent or teacher told you what you should be doing? Other than making the best mud cookies on the block, I also enjoyed teaching myself to do things. I taught myself to ride a bike, swim, roller skate, and twirl a baton. I created a sticker collection and made pins for the band I was obsessed with. I took home

11 Affirmations for Imagination

- I welcome new possibilities in my life.

- I was made to thrive, not merely survive.

- The creative opportunities that surround me are endless.

- I receive creativity in my life.

- I embrace play.

- The practical details will find a way to work out.

- I protect space in my life for imagination.

- I choose to see wonder in my own life.

- I am open to inspiration.

- I am in tune with my inner child and full of possibilities and ideas.

- I am capable of finding innovative solutions for any concerns.

Imagination Questions

- Can you picture yourself in ten or twenty years? What would you be most proud of at that point in your life?

- What did you do to play when you were a kid?

- Have you ever imagined a dream scenario for yourself that kept coming to mind?

- Do you think you give space to your imagination? Why or why not?

- Who or what helps you embrace more imagination in your life?

- If you could change something in the world and make a positive impact, what would it be?

- If money were no object, how would you spend your time?

- If you knew you could not fail, what would you do?

- What's a story, movie, or song that inspires you?

- If you could live anywhere, where would you choose and why?

- Is there something you've always wanted to learn or experiment with?

stacks of books from the library and read them from cover to cover. I was fascinated with whales. I went to the beach with my friend and we swam far past the break line, floating on boogie boards until our skin turned hot and pink. I made accessories for my Barbies in the form of doll-sized letters and home decor. I created a magazine. I made salt dough ornaments and played with my dog.

When you list these things for yourself, you may be inspired to pick something up again that you used to love, or you can find new ways to play that recreate that feeling now. What did it feel like to be energized yet relaxed? See if you can transport yourself to that time and recapture those moments of curiosity, wonder, and imagination. You're never too old to discover what play looks like in your life today.

I love hearing about ways people make space for play. Here are some things I see my friends doing in case you're looking for some ideas to get you started: playing pickleball, building LEGO sets, hiking, going to a dance class, painting, doing ceramics, making Halloween costumes from scratch, gardening, woodworking, perfecting a chocolate chip cookie recipe that is to die for, rock climbing, hosting in-home coffee shop pop-ups for friends and neighbors, making homemade hot sauce, watercolor painting, bird-watching, interior decorating, thrifting, doing puzzles, hosting board game gatherings, and joining a choir. Like your imagination, there's no limit to the possibilities.

Capitalistic Questions

Capitalistic questions put concerns about money and financial realities front and center. These questions filter all desires through the lens of financial concerns and gauge a desire's validity, worth, or importance according to how it does or does not add up monetarily. "I'm passionate about this creative endeavor, but I could never make a living doing this, so it's a waste of time."

Kim was a talented engineer who had been promoted to a manager role at her company. We met when I spoke at a retreat, and she came to me at a career crossroads, deciding whether to continue with her current role or accept an offer at a new firm. She told me she had a tendency to ignore her desires because of financial concerns. "I ask myself if I'm willing to take a 50 percent pay cut to do something I want. If not, I don't give that desire any attention and put it to the side." Kim's financial reasons for shutting her desires down reflected something many of us experience as well. With the pressing reality of bills to pay and mouths to feed, we may feel like our only choices are either paying attention to our desires or having a sustainable financial situation. We haven't been taught to reevaluate whether we might be working under a false binary.

It's tough to hold space for our desires in the capitalist reality that we live in. It's not solely an individual problem or a failure of personal character when we are overwhelmed by finances. We've inherited a broken system that's built on inequity, and we find ourselves needing to figure out how to navigate this reality. I'm a daughter of an immigrant mother who taught me how a credit card works when I was in grade school, so I'm never going to tell you to handle your finances in ways that feel irresponsible or haphazard. So, I'm not saying that financial constraints aren't real. But I am saying we can find a way to interact with our desires without capitalistic questions automatically shutting down a conversation that hasn't had a chance to begin. Learning how to navigate capitalistic questions thoughtfully gives our desires a chance to speak.

Capitalistic questions sound like:

Am I willing to become broke for this desire? If not, then it doesn't matter.

Will this desire enable me to pay my bills? If not, then I ignore it.

How does this desire relate to financial considerations?

Do I currently see a way to afford this?

Does this desire provide any monetary benefit?

Viewing your desires primarily through the lens of your finances from the get-go will make it much harder to hear your desires speak. I see a couple of problems when capitalistic questions are at the forefront. First, as a human being, you're more than what you get paid to do, and even if you have desires that won't ever pay you a dime, that doesn't automatically mean those desires are unimportant. Under capitalism, what you get paid to do is often seen as the most significant thing about you, as if a number on a pay stub could sum up a person's worth. But you can thrive in ways that have nothing to do with dollars and cents. Your inherent value as a person is not the same as what you earn, and your desires are worth listening to.

Second, when you dismiss your desires because they seem unaffordable, you might be shortchanging the process. Some things will be out of reach financially, but other times, there are creative means that we have yet to discover. It can be helpful to rethink our assumptions about what does and doesn't work.

I've come to appreciate the power of the word *maybe* and how it keeps the door of possibility cracked open. *Maybe* helps us learn to hold the tension between what we want and what is possible for a little bit longer, so we can give our desires more of a chance to say what they have to say. In the face of capitalistic questions, *maybe* can be a beautiful word that carries hopeful expectation and lets you remain open to the possibility of abundance.

When you find yourself struggling not to let finances automatically shut down your desires, try playing the Maybe Game. The finances don't work. Or maybe they will. The market is too tough. Or maybe you can start a successful business even in this market. You'll never be able to afford a vacation. Or maybe you'll find a creative way to make it happen. You'll have to suck it up and take a significant pay cut to make a lateral move. Or maybe you'll find something that both fits better and pays well. Your company doesn't have any funds for a raise. Or maybe it does. Maybe there are options you don't yet know of. Maybe you'll find the exception to the rule. Maybe you'll uncover the needle in the haystack. Someone's going to, so why not you? Maybe the finances are impossible *and* maybe there is more abundance than we think.

Last, even if something isn't financially viable, it is still worth your time to be curious about what is underneath that desire. If a super fancy vacation at a five-star resort isn't possible even though you desperately want it to be, what is the desire behind the desire? Maybe it's a desire for rest. Maybe it's a desire for beauty. Maybe it's a desire for connection with people you love. If you can identify the desire within the desire, there might be other actionable and more viable ways to engage with what you truly want, even if you don't have the lavish budget for one specific form of that desire.

Instead of capitalistic questions, ask yourself curiosity questions.

Curiosity questions allow you to challenge the assumptions that capitalistic questions often make. Curiosity tells us that any assumptions we have about money-related reasons for shutting down our desires are just that. Assumptions. And by definition, assumptions can be proven wrong just as much as they can be proven right. Can you start a business in your mid-forties after spending your entire career in the same nonprofit organization? My assumptions (not to mention other people's) told me no. What did it matter if I wanted to run my own business if it would never be financially viable? I can now happily say that those assumptions were wrong, but I didn't know it at the time, and I lived with that question for the first couple of years as I built my business.

Curiosity prevents us from saying no to our desires when the universe might have wanted to say yes. It allows us to hold space for our desires, even in light of unyielding financial realities. One of my clients described this tension perfectly when they identified a strong desire to pursue a creative passion but didn't yet know what that would mean financially, especially as they were someone with the responsibilities of caring for a young family. In the wrestling, they found a posture of curiosity that allowed room for this desire while waiting to see the financial outcomes: "I'm holding

11 Affirmations for Curiosity

- I am capable of overcoming financial obstacles.
- I welcome opportunities to experience abundance.
- I hold my desires with curiosity about how they will be realized.
- I am open to possibilities.
- I look forward to seeing how my needs will be met.
- My contributions are valuable.

- I use my resources with generosity to care for others.
- I'm grateful for the good things that flow to me.
- I cultivate a positive mindset with money.
- My needs will be taken care of in unexpected ways.
- I will be provided for in ways that I have yet to see.

Curiosity Questions

- What inspires curiosity in you?
- What helps you explore how things could be possible financially?
- What are your assumptions about what is or isn't feasible financially?
- Where do your assumptions about finances come from?
- What can you do to hold limiting assumptions more loosely?
- Who or what helps foster curiosity about potential financial obstacles for you?

- When was a time that you experienced generosity through receiving it?
- When was a time that you experienced generosity through giving it?
- When was a time that you experienced financial limitations as an opportunity for being innovative and resourceful?
- What kind of perspective would you like to have about financial concerns?
- What are stories of surprising abundance that are meaningful to you?

lightly to my hope for this desire to generate income. I want to try walking the fine line between not cutting myself off from thinking it could happen and also not assuming that it has to in order for it to be important." This is a perfect way to describe what it can look like to know that financial concerns are real but they also don't necessarily have to take the driver's seat. If more of us could learn how to do this, I think we would experience much more life and positive momentum with the things we want.

Curiosity likes to say, "Let's see," "I wonder," and you already know my personal favorite, "Maybe." Engaging in curiosity allows us to hold our negative assumptions and capitalistic questions lightly enough to create space for our desires to grow.

Permission Questions

When you feel like you aren't allowed to want what you want, permission questions are usually to blame. They tell you that you're not permitted to have the desires that you have, whether that lack of permission is implicit or explicit, actual or perceived, coming from others or yourself. These questions make you feel like there are official lists of things that are okay to want and not okay to want.

If you have a lot of permission questions, you might associate a specific authority figure, family member, or other person with the lack of permission you feel. You may notice that you picture that individual (or group of people) as an imaginary spokesperson. Sometimes it's more than just imagined, and you recall actual statements and conversations when you were told that your desires were unacceptable: "My dad always said this was frivolous, and I hear his voice when I think about it." Other times, permission questions can show up as an unspecified gut feeling that what you want is not permitted. All of this can make it feel unsafe or anxiety-producing to think about your desires. This is especially true if you feel like admitting that you want something on the not-okay list will jeopardize your relationships with people. We are relationally oriented creatures, and from an evolutionary standpoint, survival depended on being connected to others. It makes sense that our brains have been trained to fear being ostracized and to scan for social acceptance risks.

Permission questions sound like:

Do I have permission to want this? Is it *really* okay?

What would [insert person whose opinion matters to you] say about this?

Will I be judged or shamed if I am honest about what I want?

Who will be upset or angry if I say this is what I want? What would their response be?

Am I selfish, greedy, or frivolous to want this in the first place?

If the answer to any of these questions makes you feel like you don't have permission to want what you want, then you suppress your desires. Over time, repressing your desires becomes an ingrained habit, so it is much harder to hear what your desires want to say.

When Sara and I chatted, we talked about an everyday yet symbolic example of this in her life. She told me about the worn-out curtains in her living room that were torn from age and use. She hated seeing them like that day in and day out, but she also didn't feel like it was okay to want to replace them. When she tried to identify where this unease came from, she recognized how she had internalized her family's firmly held value of frugality common to those of us who grew up in immigrant families. She wrestled with what it would mean for that value if she spent money on something like a new set of curtains. She went back and forth whenever she saw the curtains and felt guilty when she noticed the desire she had to replace them. It was hard to know what to do with that strong inner voice telling her that what she wanted was unacceptable, but if she was honest, she was longing to brighten up the room and make it a more beautiful, hospitable space. Even the simple act of naming this desire for beauty was a new way to frame her desire rather than simply telling herself it was trivial.

This example highlights how confusing it can be to sort out permission questions. It is especially layered when these questions also intersect with family and cultural values. It can feel like an either-or situation. Either I honor my parents' values and don't get the curtains I want, or I do get curtains and disappoint the people I care about. A scenario in which we honor our cultural values while also having something more beautiful and functional doesn't seem possible. Sara's story highlights how something as simple as replacing curtains can bring up internal barriers and feelings about permission. Like most aspects of life, our desires are connected to other parts of us and often signify more than we realize. It's about the curtains, and it also has nothing to do with the curtains.

The problem with permission questions is that they place the locus of control outside of yourself. Permission questions set others' opinions above your own. Sometimes this happens in your own head as you project a lack of permission onto yourself, even if no one else is actually denying it to you. When this happens, your ability to listen to your desires takes a hit that's hard to overcome. If you believe you must wait for others to give you permission to want what you want, you'll hesitate to take your desires seriously. You could spend your life waiting for permission slips that may never come.

Instead of permission questions, ask yourself agency questions.

Asking questions that focus on agency rather than permission helps you focus on the truth that no one lives your life for you. No matter how much you love, admire, or fear someone, you are the one who has to live with the choices you make. Agency is not the same as individualism, which highlights individuals in isolation and ignores the collective. However, when you own your sense of agency, you know there is a central part of living your life that is for you and only you.

Only you can know what your desires are honestly saying. Only you know how joy feels in your body and soul. Only you can say what uniquely lights you up. And on the flip side, only you will experience the pain of shrinking yourself or hiding away your authentic self. One of the most common regrets of the dying is not having the courage to live true to oneself rather than the expectations of others.[4] It's deeply sad and sobering to think of coming to the end of our lives and feeling deep regret for how we lived, bound by others' opinions, but it's worth thinking about while we have time to do something about it. When you get to the end of your life, only you can judge whether you lived as your true self. Agency gently but firmly bids you not to forget these realities.

Being in touch with your agency also helps you find creative and connective ways to approach your desires. For Sara, as she considered the impasse with her living room curtains, agency gave her space to pay attention to her desire and not automatically shut it down with permission questions. She noticed that she had a tendency to be, in her words, "practical and frugal to a fault," which made it hard for her to choose things for joy, beauty, or pleasure. She came to see the choice to replace the curtains as a way to practice loving and honoring herself while also holding the value of using money well, just with more nuance. That decision became an invitation to make room for and honor herself and her desire.

About six months after our initial conversation, I saw Sara again online during a virtual workshop. Since we were on a video call, I couldn't help peeking at the window behind her to look at the curtains. A huge smile broke out on my face when I noticed that the old set was gone, and a lovely new one hung in its place. I sent her a message via chat, "It's so good to see you again, and I absolutely love the new curtains!" Again, it was never just about the curtains.

We need others, but we don't live our lives by committee, and it's not selfish to remember that. As much as I love the people in my life, and their support, perspective, and correction are invaluable to me, they will never be able to do everything I need to do to live as my true self. No partner, mentor, friend, leader, therapist, or family member can, no matter how much they love you. Agency allows you to own your desires and your journey in the way that only you can.

11 Affirmations for Agency

- I allow myself to be true to who I am.
- I give myself permission to listen to my inner guidance and follow it.
- I am wise.
- I release the judgments and criticism of others.
- I am loved, whether or not I have the approval of others.
- I'm allowed to take up space in my own life.
- I am empowered to make my own decisions.
- I don't need anyone's permission to take action.
- I am capable of discerning my unique path.
- My needs and wants are important.
- I am free to create the life that is meant for me.

Agency Questions

- What small actions can you take to connect with a sense of agency in your life?
- Who or what helps you embrace agency in your life?
- What hinders your ability to embrace agency in your life? Are there things you can let go of?
- What area of your life do you currently feel the most sense of agency in?
- What area of your life do you currently feel the least sense of agency in?
- When was a time that you experienced regret and what did you learn from that?
- What are signs that you're feeling connected to your agency?
- What are signs that you're feeling disconnected from your agency?
- What words, themes, or thoughts motivate you the most to connect to your sense of agency?
- What does it mean to you to live without regret?
- As you look ahead, how do you anticipate having a sense of agency helping you in your journey?

Learning how to recognize competency, pragmatic, capitalistic, and permission questions and see them for what they are is a significant step in making room for your desires. Once you have gained that ability, you're set up well to turn your attention to engaging with primary questions that most help you know what you want.

The Authentic Alignment Pathway

The heart of the pathway we'll use together is made up of primary questions. It teaches us how to ask them and focuses on four specific primary questions in particular. It's called the authentic alignment pathway, and each of the four stages focuses on a different central primary question. When you work through this pathway, it helps you know what your desires are, how to live them out, and how to create alignment with your authentic self.

I developed this pathway through listening to my clients' individual stories and then stepping back to hold that collection of experiences together in search of themes, principles, patterns, and best practices within them. When I did that, I found threads of commonality between seemingly disparate stories. I discovered that real-life experiences gave rise to principles and practices that in turn helped more people thrive in their day-to-day lives. The people I've worked with come from a wide variety of contexts (education, law, medicine, finance, nonprofit leadership, government, academia, science, business, local communities, and one person who was both a professional model and a data scientist). They represent a diversity of human experiences and a spectrum of faith and cultural backgrounds.

After learning from these conversations and identifying the throughlines in them, I saw the pathway tested and retested in the context of real, lived experience. Each person I've had the honor of guiding through this process has taught me something, and that learning is what I now offer to you.

Authentic Alignment Pathway		
Stage	*Name*	*Central Primary Question*
1	Calibration	What makes you come alive?
2	Expansion	How do you spark an imagination for possibilities?
3	Experimentation	How do you turn curiosity into clarity?
4	Integration	How are you being invited to exercise agency with your desires?

Stage One: Calibration

What makes you come alive?

In stage one, the central primary question asks what makes you come alive and, conversely, what does not. The calibration stage helps you grow in self-awareness about who you are by exploring your journey through an important part of our lives called peak and contrast experiences. We'll talk about what peak and contrast experiences are, how to identify them, and how to draw actionable insight from them. This stage helps you focus on the strengths, talents, and genius that are uniquely yours, so you can amplify them even more. It helps you build a personalized profile of what thriving and aliveness look like in your life, so you can calibrate the rest of the process to what is uniquely meaningful to you.

Stage Two: Expansion

How do you spark an imagination for possibilities?

In stage two, the central primary question is about how you expand your imagination for what could be. This stage asks you to consider creating an expansive approach to what you want and to do so honestly and authentically. This helps you pay attention to the possibilities that excite inspiration when you think about what you really want and how you envision living well. Expansion helps you build on the self-awareness of calibration to be able to look toward what's possible with creativity and imagination. It helps you start to answer the question of what could be out there for you and navigate uncertainty with courage to live with a healthy sense of imagination for your life.

Stage Three: Experimentation

How do you turn curiosity into clarity?

In stage three, the central primary question is focused on how to experiment with curiosity to lead you to clarity. In this stage, you learn how to not just wait for clarity to arrive but to create it for yourself. Through an enlightening but doable process of experimentation, you build a sense of what desires truly fit you from an embodied place. The experimentation stage helps you design the process, questions, and tangible steps that move you toward creating clarity about what you really want.

Stage Four: Integration

How are you being invited to exercise agency with your desires?

In stage four, the central primary question is concerned with how to exercise agency with your desires. When you're able to answer this question well, it helps you understand how to make your desires reality by finding invitations to agency without being able to control every outcome. This is vital because this process is not just about knowing what you want but also finding your best, most authentic ways of acting on your desires. This stage teaches you about being adaptable and responsive in the process of bringing your desires to life. Integration focuses on the art of weaving what you want with real-life outcomes and learning to navigate all the beauty and complexity of this important stage. It teaches you how to embrace a sense of agency within the realities we face when we set out to live in greater alignment with what we want.

In each stage, we'll examine one central primary question and discuss why it matters. We'll also look at the practical side of answering that question within the context of your life, including specific steps to discover meaningful personal insight. As its name implies, the authentic alignment pathway is not one-size-fits-all and needs to be tailored to your true self and the unique way that will be expressed. Each stage of the pathway works with the others to help you create clarity and momentum around your desires.

Go at Your Own Pace

When you walk along a trail, you don't walk at the same pace as everyone else who is on the trail that day too. Inevitably, there are people who are going faster or slower than you. You make adjustments for that by letting those going a faster pace pass you or vice versa. You'll have a better experience if you stay focused on the pace that is right for you.

It's the same with learning to take steps toward clarity and finding your way through the primary and secondary questions in your life. Your process is unique to you, and the pace at which you discover clarity will differ from someone else's. I've seen people who naturally go through the stages at a quick pace and find clarity through the pathway within a fairly short period of time. I've seen others whose pace is slower and steady, so it takes more time for the answers to unfold. I'd put myself in the slower category, as it felt like it took more time for me to navigate my way to the clarity and alignment that was right for me.

So, hold your expectations about your process with a lot of openness, and remember that it's more important to progress along the path than to go at a certain pace. We have control over the steps we take toward alignment, but the timing of how everything comes together can be a mystery. Perfect timing is whatever pace is right for you. In the meantime, be curious with your questions, be gentle with yourself, and keep going with trust that each consistent step will make the rest of the path clearer.

───────────┤ **REFLECTION PROMPT** ├───────────

Question Parking Lot

The poet Rainer Maria Rilke wrote, "Be patient toward all that is unsolved in your heart and try to love the questions themselves, like locked rooms and like books that are now written in a very foreign tongue."[5] Loving the questions themselves teaches us how to be people who are able to stay open to our desires in both the solved and unsolved parts of knowing what we want. Creating a question parking lot helps you acknowledge the questions you're asking, both primary and secondary, and gives you a place to set them down for now. In doing so, you create distance from any unhelpful questions, so their chaos doesn't take over your ability to listen to your desires. Putting them in the parking lot for safekeeping allows you to come back to them when they can be helpful rather than disruptive. This gives you more room to engage with primary questions in your life.

Step One: Specify your questions.

The first step is to do a brain dump of all the questions that you have when you think about what you want. Write down the questions that you notice going through your head and how those questions make you feel. You can refer back to the four types of questions (competency, pragmatic, capitalistic, and permission) to give you some ideas to spur your reflection. Remember that you can always change this list or add to it, so don't feel like you need to get it exactly perfect or overthink what you put down. Like all of the reflection prompts, this is dynamic, and you can change it as much as you need to.

Step Two: Identify where you're at.

Take a moment to notice how it feels to see your questions in written form. Sometimes people say it is a relief to give those questions a place to live outside their minds, and they feel some of the weight of those questions lifted off their shoulders. Other times, the process can create the opposite feeling. What's your experience as you look at the questions you've written down? Do you feel relieved, overwhelmed, or something else?

Also, notice what category of question you're holding. What type(s) of questions do you have the most of? Are they mostly primary or secondary questions? If they're secondary questions, which type? If you notice that you have questions that don't fit into any of the categories, feel free to write those down too.

Step Three: Park the questions symbolically.

Last, release your questions. The simple act of writing them down might be enough for you to let go of these questions, at least for the time being. Some people find it helpful to create a simple ritual as an external marker of this inner change. For example, you could fold the page over to cover them for now, signifying your intention to release these questions so you can be more attentive to what your desires have to say. You can also talk about the questions with someone else as a way to further process them.

You can finish this exercise by taking a few deep, cleansing breaths. As you breathe in, you're breathing in oxygen for your desires, space for yourself, and anything else you need. As you breathe out, you're releasing fear, self-criticism, anxiety, and anything else you need to let go of. Let this be an act of trust for what's to come.

It's unlikely that all your questions will automatically disappear. That doesn't mean that you've failed somehow. It just means that they are a natural part of the process that you're in. You can return to this exercise whenever new questions emerge or you need a reminder not to let secondary questions take over.

QUESTION PARKING LOT

Write down all the questions that come to mind when you ask what you really want.	How does it feel to see your questions written out?
	Are your questions mostly primary or secondary questions? If they are secondary, what type (competency, pragmatic, capitalistic, permission)?
	How will you release your secondary questions for now?

PART 2

The AUTHENTIC ALIGNMENT PATHWAY

4

Stage One: Calibration

*Coming Alive, Peak Experiences,
and Your Unique Inner Compass*

R uth was at a turning point in her career, and when we met for our first coaching call, she angled her video camera toward the wall behind her desk to show me several large pieces of poster paper filled with thoughts and questions that arose when she tried to name what she wanted for the next season of her life. It was impressively thorough, but understandably overwhelming, because it was too much to juggle all at once. Together, we talked through the questions that had been swirling around her and identified the secondary questions that could be parked for now to give her space to focus on primary questions instead. Ruth was ready to begin working through the authentic alignment pathway and to start with stage one: calibration.

In calibration, the primary question is, What makes you come alive? This stage is about learning to notice and understand aliveness because when you pay attention to what aliveness means in your life, you're able to create more of it in the future. The fact that this question comes first in the pathway is significant. Starting with the question of aliveness ensures that the rest of the process and subsequent stages are centered on the core intention of creating alignment in your life, keeping that in mind from the start.

Sometimes when people struggle to know what they want, it's because they've become disconnected from an embodied, aligned sense of themselves. They don't know what they really want because they don't know enough about who they really are. Starting with calibration keeps us from approaching the process in a way that won't ultimately be aligned with who we are. It focuses on what thriving should look like in your life, not a generic template. It makes sure that the rest of the journey is centered on what fits you.

I first encountered the idea of aliveness through esteemed theologian and civil rights leader Howard Thurman. One of his most well-known and beloved quotes is a beautiful and powerful plea for learning to come alive: "Don't ask what the world needs. Ask what makes you come alive, and go do it. Because what the world needs is people who have come alive."[1] His words are often quoted and shared because they capture a deep longing, which many of us have, to live a vibrant life and to believe our aliveness can make a difference in the world. He offers us an inspiring vision of how our thriving and impact can be interconnected, and he points us to the hope that perhaps our lives hold some of the answers to the questions the world is asking.

Thurman's famous words inspire me every time I read them. However, their purpose isn't simply to sound eloquent. His words have the power to galvanize us to live out the aliveness that he talks about and to remember that when this happens, its magic is transformative.

A little while after my forty-day experiment ended, I decided to get certified in coaching. To complete the training, I needed to coach some real people who would evaluate me if I wanted the official piece of paper saying I was legitimately certified. Through an accidental miscommunication on my part, I ended up with seven times more volunteers than I needed for that portion of the process. I only needed five people, but I found thirty-five willing volunteers who were ready to help me out by doing some free coaching together.

Rather than deciding to turn people away, I chose to meet with everyone. Ever the sucker for a good learning experience, I couldn't help but be curious to see what I would discover from talking to as many people as I could. On some days, I had five or six calls in a row, and my fears about it being a waste of time didn't last long because I quickly discovered how much I loved it. The coaching conversations felt so energizing that I found myself dancing in the hallways of my house before and after calls, as if the joy in my body needed an outlet. One day, my husband came home from work and asked me how my day went, and when I recounted the full day of five back-to-back calls, I began to dance all over again. After the low of the VP job rejection, I felt more energy than I'd felt in months and like a part of me I hadn't seen in a long time was coming to life again.

This experience was a master class in aliveness. It helped me understand what this amazing-sounding concept actually looks like when it's being lived out. It's one thing to read words about coming alive, be moved by them, or admire others who embody aliveness, but this was a moment that taught me what aliveness looks and feels like in my life through an embodied knowing. I also learned to notice the conditions that were a part of creating that experience in my life, and how connecting with people this way felt like me showing up as my most alive, authentic self. I discovered a deep desire and passion for helping people understand their stories and embrace their capacity for goodness, creativity, and leadership that also makes me want to dance up and down the hallways on a random Wednesday. I was eager to see if this could be more than a one-time event and to test how I might use it as a template for seeking future joy. Howard Thurman told me to value aliveness. My life and my desires taught me how to chase it.

I now have the incredible privilege of helping people uncover their own stories of aliveness. It is magical to watch people describe their personal version of dancing in hallways and the ways they come alive. Listening to these experiences is by far one of my favorite things about what I get to do.

Have you ever noticed how someone changes when they talk about the things that make them come alive? Their body language becomes more animated. Their faces light up. They literally look more alive. They say words like *fun, energizing,* and *life-giving*. When you hear someone talking about one of these moments, the energy around them changes. When aliveness shows up in our lives, it's visceral and sacred.

So, what is aliveness, and what is it not? How do we define it? In nature, when something is alive, it is nourished and fed from within, and growth happens from the inside out. Similarly for us, being alive is a state of living with an inner sense of authentic well-being that comes through in vibrant, fruitful ways. Aliveness happens when we are aligned with our true selves, one another, the values that are most meaningful to us, and the divine. Aliveness cannot exist in a disembodied state; it must exist in the grounded, lived reality of who we are. It comes from the experience of uncovering how we're meant to thrive and be the essence of the kind of people the world needs most.

Aliveness Is More Than Performance

Most of us group everything that we do well in a single category in our head. We tend not to differentiate between what we're capable of doing and what truly makes us come alive. We call all of it "our strengths." But performance and aliveness are different things, and if you technically do something well but you are drained by it or dread it, that's not aliveness. The abilities you have to perform, be successful, or deliver results are useful, but they shouldn't be interchangeable with what truly lights you up. If you do something well but you feel depleted by it, that's a competency but not aliveness. It can be tempting to focus solely on competencies because they often come with external validation, but it's important to be clear about the difference between mere competency and true aliveness. Aliveness comes when we do something well and we find it deeply life-giving. Most of us would benefit from being more specific in how we talk about our strengths and distinguishing aliveness from performance.

Jason was beginning to notice this distinction in his life. For some time, he'd been confused about his experience of leading staff meetings. He valued these meetings because he knew they were strategic. People gave him heartfelt positive feedback about the way he led them. But Jason's internal experience was that leading these meetings took a lot out of him in a way that other parts of his role did not. It was a skill and an important competency, but it wasn't tapping into aliveness. Being able to make that distinction helped Jason notice where aliveness was and wasn't, even while others praised the fantastic job he was doing.

Aliveness should only be reserved for the times when you both do something well and feel great while doing it. When that distinction isn't clear enough in your mind, you may be inadvertently creating the perfect conditions for your own burnout. Doing things that make you feel alive can be scary or challenging, but that's not the same thing as feeling depleted, drained, or worn out by them. Learn to pay attention to the difference between competency and aliveness in your life.

Aliveness Is Not Universal

One of the most important things to understand about aliveness is that it is highly specific to each one of us. The way you come alive is unique. When someone hasn't considered this truth, the default assumption is that the way they come alive is the same as everyone else. The problem with this line of thinking is that it causes them to take their own aliveness for granted. I've lost track of the number of times I have had a person talk about a beautiful experience of joy and aliveness that I've never heard anybody else express in quite the same way, only to have them conclude, "Yeah, but anybody could have done the same thing," when nothing could be further from the truth.

Aliveness and the way that it comes through you is unique. When you discover aliveness in your life, please know that you've found something incredibly rare. In fact, Gallup, an organization that studies human potential and talent, has a popular assessment called CliftonStrengths that is used to help people identify their strengths and what they do best. According to their research, the odds that you'll have the same strengths as someone else is a staggering one in thirty-three million chance.[2]

I saw an example of this one day when I had back-to-back meetings with individual clients. The first client told me about how much she loved event planning and running thoughtful, engaging, and excellent events that created a positive experience for attendees and served the host's goals. It brought her so much joy, and she thrived in the whole process, before, during, and after an event.

Thirty minutes later, I was talking to another client who told me how much she hated event planning and how she would be more than happy never to be in charge of planning another event again in her life. She talked about how much she loved mentoring people one-on-one instead, and how that was where she felt she shined. She loved walking other people through a relational process of development and growth.

I wished these two individuals could hear each other talking about their encounters with aliveness, so they could understand how unique their stories were and that not everyone experienced it as they did. Put it this way—for everything you love doing and feel is your version of coming alive, I guarantee dozens of other people have told me how much they hate doing that same thing.

Do you enjoy planning a special event like a party, shower, or celebration for your loved ones? Do you love sitting with data or numbers to find the patterns that emerge from them? Do you delight in thinking through a hard-to-solve problem until you spot the best solution? Are you excellent at holding teams accountable to do what they said they would and to act in ways that uphold the integrity of their stated values? Do you adore talking to strangers and see everyone around you as a potential new friend? Or would you rather spend an afternoon in meaningful conversation with an important person in your life, furthering a deep connection with them? Do you thrive in new situations where you fully admit you have no idea what you are doing? Do you lift the energy of a room when you walk into it and make everyone else feel more positive about being together? Do you easily spot routes forward and identify how to address needed mid-course adjustments? Do you come alive when you teach, mentor, lead, think deeply, learn, strategize, plan, bring others together, build community, write, speak, organize, create, brainstorm, plan, think ahead, rally others, or problem-solve? When you notice the unique way that aliveness shows up in your life, know that it does not happen in quite the same way for anyone else.

Aliveness Can Be Easy to Miss

Because of all of this, it's easy to take aliveness for granted. It's far too easy to overlook what uniquely makes you come alive, assume that anybody else could do what comes easily to you, overvalue external markers of success, or focus solely on your weaknesses and what you lack. But research on the science of human flourishing shows that you are much more likely to say that you experience a high quality of life when you learn to focus on the unique way that you come alive.[3] This field is known as positive psychology because of its emphasis on the positive aspects of human potential rather than pathologies. It has been shaped by scientists like Abraham Maslow, Martin Seligman, and Mihaly Csikszentmihalyi.

After majoring in English in college, Tâm had built a successful career in finance and was thinking about the next step. Even though she'd clearly been able to accomplish a lot, she didn't always have the ability to notice or articulate what she did uniquely well and what made her come alive. She told me about an interview experience in which she sent personal thank-you notes not only to the people who conducted the interview but also the receptionist who had helped her get set up. We talked about her thoughtful attention to people, relational skills, and the way she both enjoyed and excelled at building relationships. But it had been easy for her to take it for granted based on the assumption that everyone could do what came to her so naturally. As we worked together, Tâm made a practice to journal on a weekly basis about what she saw come out of her strengths as a way of noticing and understanding what made her come alive. Over time, she saw how much more clarity and intentionality she had about what did and did not contribute to her aliveness.

Far too few people have the curiosity it takes to understand their own aliveness in a way that makes a meaningful difference in how they live. Being curious about your aliveness isn't about egotism, arrogance, or a feeling of superiority to others. A deep, ongoing curiosity about what aliveness means to you helps you identify your desires and expand your imagination for your life. Don't miss your own aliveness.

Discovering Aliveness in Your Peak Experiences and Contrast Experiences

If you want to understand what your unique aliveness looks like, you have access to the most valuable primary source material you could ever ask for—your own life. If you want to create aliveness tomorrow, the best place to start is by looking at where it already happened yesterday. Your lived experience contains pure gold for uncovering powerful insight about how you come alive and what you can do to create more aliveness. Excavating the beauty contained in your life gives you access to the unsurpassed self-awareness that's a nonnegotiable for understanding what alignment will mean in your life. Harvard-trained neuroscientist Juliette Han calls self-awareness the most underestimated ability linked to success, creativity, better decision-making, and building stronger relationships.[4]

Everyone has significant lived experiences that, when understood, help reveal important truth about how they come alive. I call these your peak experiences and contrast experiences. Even though everyone has these experiences, not everyone has learned to notice or interpret them.

Peak experiences are specific examples in your life of the times when you felt like you were most alive, and they help you identify what contributed to that feeling. As we have talked about, these are the instances when you not only did something well but also really enjoyed it. When people talk about their peak experiences, you feel joy emanating from them. *I loved doing this. I felt so energized. This was so much fun. I can't wait to do this again.* Peak experiences reveal what is most motivating, energizing, and life-giving to you. They may have come with praise, success, or other types of external validation, but the most important thing to pay attention to is the presence of energy and aliveness that you feel within. When I did the thirty-five coaching calls that made me dance down my hallway, I discovered a new and meaningful peak experience in my life.

Examples of peak experiences that people have shared include:

- Training for and competing in a Tough Mudder, an extreme boot camp–style obstacle course with pits of mud and barbed wire
- Planning a conference that was meaningful and impactful, alongside a team that loved working together
- Writing a speech and giving it to an important gathering of influential stakeholders
- Hosting a thoughtful, personalized wedding shower for a best friend
- Creating a clear and actionable professional development plan for a new team member
- Coordinating an annual camping trip for a reunion of friends
- Being a mentor for someone else and investing in their growth
- Running the editorial team of a school newspaper

- Leading a team to create genuine community and collaboration
- Starting a cake-making business
- Producing a concert for a community
- Caring well for a beloved aging family member
- Creating a system of financial equity and transparency across an entire organization

Conversely, contrast experiences are the opposite of peak experiences. They are times when you did something that was draining or depleting, even if you did a good job performance-wise. If it was something that you had to do for an extended period of time, you may have come to dread it. People describe these experiences very differently than peak experiences. *People told me I did well, but I felt so drained afterward. I dread doing this kind of thing. This took so much out of me. I'd be happy to never do this again.* Contrast experiences show you the types of things that work against your aliveness. They show you what is not for you and what will be important to limit or avoid in order to protect space for the things that do make you come alive.

When you understand your peak and contrast experiences, it helps you calibrate your inner compass. Just as a needle of a compass is attracted or repelled by the earth's natural magnetism, the unique magnetism of your inner compass helps you navigate your life toward the contexts, places, and experiences that will foster your aliveness and away from the ones that don't. In other words, you help tune in to your inner compass when you understand your peak and contrast experiences so they can show you what is for you and what isn't. This calibration helps you create genuine alignment between your desires and your life. The more you learn to pay attention to this inner compass, the more finely tuned it becomes, guiding you in the process of discovering your desires and thriving.

If you don't think you have any of these experiences, it's usually because you haven't learned to notice them, and you may have moved on from them too quickly to spot them. Everyone has peak and contrast experiences, but you may need some additional prompting and space to figure out what they are. If this doesn't come quickly at first, remember that, as with any other skill, you'll get better at it the more you practice.

How to Calibrate Based on Your Peak and Contrast Experiences

Learning to study your own peak and contrast experiences equips you to find the treasure buried in your life. It shows you how to be calibrated to your soul's unique version of aliveness. This is invaluable for learning how to create a life that is grounded in what makes you who you are.

When you go to the beach, you might see people with metal detectors. If you're not familiar, these devices are engineered to give an alert when they sense the presence of metal. People use them at places like the beach in hopes that the sand is hiding treasures. I presume they are looking for lost jewelry or other valuable items. When the device alerts the person, they know to stop and look more closely at that specific area. They dig until they locate that item and hopefully uncover something precious. Having a device like this makes what would otherwise be an impossible task much more feasible because without it, it would be overwhelming to randomly guess where in the vast beach there might be a lost gem.

Peak and contrast experiences are like the alerts that show you where there is gold in your life, waiting to be found. They contain a treasure trove of clues as to what aliveness uniquely looks like in your life. They reveal insight and wisdom about who you have been created to be that nothing else can hold a candle to, and they also show how you can go about creating aliveness in the future. I believe that learning how to identify, analyze, and generate meaningful insight from your peak and contrast experiences is one of the most pivotal things you can do to create aliveness in your life.

You're probably already familiar with some skills needed to analyze these experiences. Remember when you were in English classes and spent time learning how to engage in literary analysis and critical thinking skills to understand books, stories, and poetry? If you're like most students, you probably had to do a fair amount of interpretation, character and plot analysis, and theme exploration. You may think that you were only learning how to break down *Romeo and Juliet* and *The House on Mango Street*, but, in reality, you were also gaining some essential skills for understanding the peak and contrast experiences in your life. You can thank your English teacher later.

Each peak experience and contrast experience is an opportunity to learn more about what aliveness does and does not look like in your life. The more you can deeply dive into your personalized set of peak and contrast experiences, the more precise the picture you can paint of yourself and your desires. Over time, this is how you learn to create and sustain your unique paths to thriving.

Asking you to apply literary analysis energy to your experiences may sound like I'm inviting you to nerd out on your own life, and if so, it's because I am. I'd love for you to be engrossed in the details of your stories, experiences, and life because, as we've already said, this will give you the best foundation for understanding and creating aliveness in the future. (Don't worry if you don't happen to be a fan of literary analysis. This practice tends to be much more irresistibly interesting and relevant when it's about you and your life.)

Analyzing your peak experiences and contrast experiences flows from the same three steps: name, notice, and categorize. Each step helps you study your peak and contrast experiences so you can better understand not only the experience itself but also what it means for your life.

Three Steps to Reflect on Your Peak and Contrast Experiences

Step One: Name your experiences.

Step Two: Notice the details.

Step Three: Categorize your insight.

We'll talk about each step and why it's important, and in the reflection prompt at the end of the chapter, you'll get the chance to practice by thinking about your peak and contrast experiences.

Step One: Name your peak and contrast experiences.

The first step is to identify your experiences. I usually invite people to start with their peak experiences first and then move to contrast experiences later. I recommend listing three to five experiences for each category. Thinking about multiple experiences in each category gives you the opportunity to compare and contrast them. The experiences in each category can be similar or different from one another, but each one adds a different layer of understanding.

Peak and contrast experiences are everywhere; they can be found in any realm of your life in endlessly creative ways. They can come from personal or professional contexts, and one is not more important than the other. These experiences could have happened very recently or quite a long time ago. They might have been very brief—one shared example lasted only fifteen minutes—or they could have taken place over a long span of time, even multiple years. Don't rule out a potential peak or contrast experience by any particular timeline, duration, context, or other specific detail. The essential, nonnegotiable quality is for the experience to have been life-giving and to have sparked joy for you if you're thinking about peak experiences, or to have been draining and depleting if you're thinking about contrast experiences. The quality of your inner experience and energy is the most important aspect to pay attention to.

Sometimes people think it's better to be more general, but I encourage you to be as specific as you can. For example, "Mentoring Daniel while we worked on X project together for one year" is going to be better than simply writing down "Mentoring." If you've acted as a mentor dozens of times, but there's a specific mentoring relationship that is a high-light for you, that tends to be the kind of thing that is worth paying attention to. "Speaking for the board presentation when I presented the annual strategic plan" is preferable to just "Speaking." "Planning a hiking trip with my three closest friends" is better than simply "Traveling." You get the idea. After you have listed a few peak experiences and contrast experiences, you're ready to move to the next step. If this first step feels hard, give it your best shot, and don't overthink it. You can always come back to edit your list. In fact, that is encouraged.

Step Two: Notice the details.

For each peak or contrast experience, recall at least five specific details. Sometimes it helps to reimagine the experience in your mind and see what you notice by placing yourself back into that point in time. If it feels overwhelming to do this with each peak or contrast experience on your list, begin with one or two, choosing whatever feels the most interesting or fun to unpack at this time.

Remember that no detail is too small to matter. Recently, a friend and I signed up for a botanical art class for beginners. During the class, the instructor emphasized the importance of noticing the details of the leaf we were drawing. She told us to pay attention to the world of details that live in just a single leaf. I immediately saw her point when she showed us what she meant: the color of the leaf, the exact shade of green, how the light bounced off the glossiness of it, the winding veins, how it attached to the stem, and even the imperfections, patches of brown, and tears that each told an entire story. Until I stopped to notice, I had never considered how much detail there is in each leaf, though I've probably walked by countless leaves like it before. There's so much beautiful detail to notice in your experiences, and it's worth taking a closer look at them.

When you are looking for details that stand out to you, a great place to start is the main questions of journalism—who, what, when, where, why, and how. For further investigation, here are some questions I'm always interested in when asking someone to describe their peak or contrast experience:

Did you have the experience by yourself or in collaboration with others?

If the experience was with others, was that positive or negative? What qualities or actions of other people contributed to this feeling? What role did others play, and what was it like to connect with them?

What was your process like?

How did you become inspired or get the idea to do this?

What did you do specifically? What actions did you take?

Did you create a plan, and how did you come up with it?

Or were you spontaneous and improvisational in your approach?

What questions did you ask yourself?

What kind of environment did this take place in, and how did that impact your experience?

Did you have this experience in a specific geographical location, or were you working with a specific organization, issue, or context?

Why was this experience particularly motivating and satisfying if it was a peak experience?

Why was this experience particularly draining and depleting if it was a contrast experience?

What was most meaningful to you about this experience?

Did other people give you feedback that resonated with you? What did they say?

What were the outcomes and how did they compare to your expectations?

You don't have to answer every question or be exhaustive, especially if it feels tedious. Feel free to choose the questions that feel the most helpful to you. I'll also add: pay extra attention to how this experience felt in your body. If it was a peak experience, how did you feel energized, joyful, or in the flow? Even now, as you remember it, you might notice that you feel lighter and happier, as people often do when they recall their peak experiences. If it was a contrast experience, how did you feel drained or frustrated? Did you experience that sensation in a specific body part, like a heaviness at the bottom of your stomach or a tightness in your shoulders? Sometimes people name specific physical reactions that they associate with either peak or contrast experiences, and paying attention to that is also important.

Occasionally, people have a hard time coming up with a list of peak experiences and ask me how to know if they genuinely enjoyed something. This often happens for people who are highly responsible and attuned to the needs and wants of others, which means it can be hard to know if something was a peak experience because they genuinely enjoyed it or if it was something they did out of a sense of responsibility. If that's the case for you, and you're someone who has heavily prioritized duties and responsibilities in the past, look for peak experiences where your hard work and diligence were in a supporting role toward something else that was joyful or motivating to you.

Step Three: Categorize your insight.

After you have named and noticed the details of your peak or contrast experience, there is a final step that will allow you to organize your thinking and connect it to what this particular experience reveals about who you are. This is what helps you take an individual peak or contrast experience and learn from it so that it isn't just an isolated event from your past.

Cognitive psychologists call this metacognition, which essentially means you're thinking about your own thought processes. Doing this helps you learn from the experience in such a way that you'll be able to translate that insight into the future, even if the situations and contexts that await you are different from the past experience you're reflecting on. It gives you wisdom about yourself that you'll be able to utilize in future scenarios.

For example, my husband had a meaningful peak experience during his time in high school. When he was a junior, a teacher invited him to manage the student store. He took an unpopular, poorly run student store and turned it around and made it the student body's favorite place on campus. It went so well that the official school cafeteria filed a complaint because students stopped wanting to eat there, choosing to get their lunch at the student store instead. When he categorizes that experience, he identifies his love for problem-solving and taking something that isn't working very well and helping it become excellent. Because he classifies the experience metacognitively as an example of his problem-solving strength, it means he can apply that insight in his present-day life. He doesn't have to go back to high school to recreate the aliveness he experienced then. He can look for the problems in life or work today that spark his interest and creativity the most.

Here are a few more examples of categorization, using the scenarios mentioned in step one. A peak experience of mentoring could point to a love of seeing potential in others and helping them develop. Speaking for the board presentation could reveal a love of crafting and communicating a compelling message, and a gift of connecting with others. Planning a hiking trip with three close friends could show a strength in creating memorable and meaningful experiences or a love of setting up a thoughtful and thorough plan centered on important relationships.

This is a step of interpretation. It allows you to expand the learning from that initial experience to listen for what it says about who you are. What does that experience tell you about yourself? What does it say about your natural and best ways of showing up? Or by contrast, what does it say about your most difficult and unnatural ways of showing up?

One small caveat, though, is to not simplify too broadly in the categories. Here's an example of what this could look like. When I talked to Sehee, she said, "People have always told me that I'm a good listener, so I should become a therapist. So many people have told me this that I've lost count." But when I asked her whether that was something she wanted to do, her answer was an emphatic no. Sehee did have a genuine strength in being able to listen well and hold space for others, but what the well-meaning advice from people in her life didn't take into account is that becoming a therapist is only one option for how she could utilize that strength. It's an oversimplification to say that everyone who is a good listener should become a therapist. They might love to hold space for friends and family but not want to do so in a professional context. They might not have an interest or strength in navigating trauma, and instead be drawn to other types of topics or questions. In Sehee's case, she wanted to use her listening skills to lead teams, be a great manager, and work with others in a number of different ways that didn't have to do with being a therapist. So, in this step, focus on what your experiences tell you about who you are, but remember that you can apply that insight in a lot of different ways, and this is what we'll work on in subsequent stages of the pathway.

This caution about overgeneralizing applies to contrast experiences too. One night when my son was young, he was sitting at the kitchen counter working on his math homework. He got frustrated with a problem he was struggling with and didn't have a good grasp on what was going wrong. (I was not much help either, given the fact that the way they taught math when I was in elementary school was completely different.) In his frustration, he made a comment about hating math. I tried to listen to and assure him that it's natural to feel upset, but I also told him that this unit working on how to multiply fractions is only one specific math skill, and that he had loved geometry and other units. Overgeneralizing about math based on one lesson wasn't helpful or true. He begrudgingly agreed that he didn't hate all math, but he definitely hated this homework assignment. When you find a contrast experience, notice if you hate that thing in all cases and at all times, or whether your aversion to it is about something narrower and more specific. Trust what you find but don't generalize in unhelpful ways.

In this step, a tool such as a personality assessment can lend clarity and offer categories that better articulate what you're noticing about yourself without becoming too narrow, too quickly. I typically utilize an assessment tool such as CliftonStrengths, Working Genius, or the Enneagram to provide another lens to view a peak or contrast experience because I find that personality frameworks give language to dynamics, traits, or preferences that you have but might not have put to words yet. These types of assessments can be an excellent way to get you thinking or help you notice more specificity or nuance than you would have been able to see on your own.

There are many options (including Myers-Briggs, DiSC, Hogan, Birkman, Enneagram, CliftonStrengths, Working Genius, Four Tendencies, VIA, CoreClarity, Predictive Index, etc.), with new ones probably being created as we speak. If you're new to these but think one might help you, I recommend CliftonStrengths as an accessible option that is helpful for many people if you don't mind paying a fee to do it and spending a little time learning the specific terminology the assessment uses. It's not strictly necessary, but I don't do a peak and contrast experience reflection without including this aspect. Chances are you've already done something like this before and have some of your past results filed away. This can be a great opportunity to take those out, refamiliarize yourself with them, and utilize the insight in your findings to better understand what your peak and contrast experiences are saying not just about what you did in the past but where you might want to go in the future.

Remember that this initial list of core peak and contrast experiences is something you can return to, especially when you discover new ones in time that you want to add to your list, giving you additional clarity and nuance that a one-time reflection won't. Some of my clients return to it periodically, like an annual checkup to recalibrate as they continue learning and growing. In fact, this reflection becomes more robust the more you come back to it and allow yourself to continue learning from these types of experiences. I confess that I hope this will be an area of lifelong learning for you. Understanding your peak and contrast experiences throughout your journey will give you eyes to continue to find the unique beauty and wisdom in your own stories.

REFLECTION PROMPT

Understanding Your Peak and Contrast Experiences

As you begin creating your collection of stories, it's important to be open to what you find in your peak and contrast experiences. Don't censor anything. Don't dismiss a peak experience because you don't think it's significant enough. If it brought you life and joy, it matters. On the other hand, don't apologize or feel bad about a contrast experience because you think it's something you should've enjoyed. If something drains you, it doesn't say something negative about you. It probably just means it wasn't a good fit. Don't edit yourself. Trust what your life is telling you.

Part One: Peak experiences.

1. **Name:** What are three to five peak experiences that come to mind for you?
2. **Notice:** For each one, what are five specific details about what that experience was like?
3. **Categorize:** What part of you (a specific characteristic, value, trait, strength, talent, ability, genius, or gift) is this peak experience coming from?

Part Two: Contrast experiences.

1. **Name:** What are three to five contrast experiences that come to mind for you?
2. **Notice:** For each one, what are five specific details about what that experience was like?
3. **Categorize:** What part of you (a specific characteristic, value, trait, strength, talent, ability, genius, or gift) is this contrast experience conflicting with?

Part Three: Your unique inner compass.

1. Do you notice connections between your peak and contrast experiences?
2. How do peak and contrast experiences register in your body?
3. What is one takeaway that you're learning about yourself from this exercise?

Your peak and contrast experiences will help you pay attention to the specific ways that aliveness does and does not happen for you. Let them teach you new ways to think about yourself and find clarity about the unique way you show up in the world.

5

Stage Two: Expansion

Abundance, Uncertainty,
and Making Room for Possibilities

n the last chapter, we talked about paying attention to your experiences as a way to be attuned to your inner compass, and why this is beautiful and necessary in light of the unique way each of us comes to life. But, to state the obvious, the purpose of a compass is to help you go somewhere. More specifically, it's made to help you go off the beaten path. No compass is needed for the places you're already well acquainted with. You don't need a compass to go to the same grocery store you've been to a hundred times. The only reason a compass becomes necessary is if you're going somewhere unfamiliar and uncharted, where your normal routines don't apply. You only need a compass when you're going somewhere wild.

In expansion, we look to the wilderness of what might be waiting for us beyond what we currently know. We put our attention toward intentionally cultivating our ideas with openness about what's possible and the new journeys that might be ahead. If calibration gives us a compass, expansion gives us the imagination for where that compass can take us. We do this by interrogating the restrictions we've knowingly or unknowingly put around our desires and expanding our sense of what is possible beyond those limitations. In expansion, the primary question is, How do you spark an imagination for possibilities? This stage helps us create a more expansive imagination.

Sometimes venturing out into the wilderness sounds wonderful, and it's liberating to consider dreams of what could be. I remember one client, a mom of young kids, who had gone through several life and career transitions in a short period of time. When we connected, she felt like she was finally stepping into a new point in her life where she had the capacity to ask herself questions about what her desires might be saying and pointing her to. She teared up as she talked about her heartfelt gratitude for "being able to ask questions about possibilities for the first time in a long time." For her and others like her, opening up expansive space for possibilities can feel like a cherished gift.

Other times, thinking about the wilderness doesn't feel so great at all. It can feel scary and cause our resistance and apprehension to go on high alert. In theory, it should sound great to run with what could be possible for our lives, but the reality is that the process depends on a variety of factors. I've observed that it's often more common than we think to find it difficult to embrace an expansive mindset. It can feel challenging to not minimize ourselves and what we think is possible. It's also not easy to wrestle with limiting thoughts, feelings, and narratives. Here are some of the things people have said to me when confronted with the invitation to think about possibilities in an expansive way:

Sounds hard.
Just thinking about this makes me want to cry.
Seems informative but really depressing.
Uh, why does this feel so scary?
No.

When resistance like this happens, it's usually because we have unconscious limits around our desires, and we've become accustomed to living within those constraints. Over time, it's easiest and most comfortable to consistently put restrictions on our desires. We downplay what we think is possible, and minimization becomes the default mode. We might not even be aware that we're doing it to begin with. Expansion is necessary because it directs us to consider our relationship to limitations, imagination, and the boxes that we may have placed our desires in. Living with harsh limits on what seems possible doesn't feel great, but if that's what you're used to, it might just feel safe. It's hard to remember that the wilderness is good when it's just so *wild*.

Restrictions in the Wilderness

Because of this, whether your reaction to heading into the wilderness with your desires is one of deep joy and gratitude, fear and hesitation, or something in between, most of us can benefit from a conscious examination of the limitations we've fallen into the habit of living with in regard to our desires and what could be possible.

What's the line between possibility and impossibility? Some limits are ones we have falsely created. Some limits are quite real. And it's not always easy to figure out where the difference lies. It's not as simple as telling yourself to pretend that nothing is ever impossible, because clearly that's not true. It's also not helpful to assume that nothing we want is ever possible, like the person who told me, "You want me to list all the things I can't have in life? No thanks." It's a difficult part of the human experience to learn how to navigate this part of life well, staying hopeful about possibilities while not oversimplifying the reality of our lives as limited beings. But when it comes to our desires, there are several categories of limitations that are helpful to reexamine with healthy skepticism.

Limitations about Our Abilities

As we talked about with competency questions in chapter 3, it's easy to focus on how we fall short and to place strong limitations on how we see our abilities. Making space for your desires often asks you to trust that when you see a desire in your life, you have what it takes to see that desire through. Be skeptical of what you've told yourself you can and can't do, especially when you see a desire on the other side of that self-proclaimed limitation.

Limitations from Others

Other limitations to be suspicious of are edicts and declarations we receive from others. Sometimes we internalize limitations that other people have spoken over us without taking the time to examine them. For example, I think about how common it is for many young adults to be told by teachers, parents, or others that their dreams are impossible, whether it's where they want to go to school, what kind of career they want to have, or the kind of life they want to lead. I recently heard a story of a young man reflecting on how a teacher told him he'd never be able to make it as a writer, but that's exactly what he became. Thankfully, he found his way to prove this naysayer wrong, but not everyone does. Like him, be willing to take a second look at these types of internalized statements.

Limitations of Perspective

Lastly, some of us have cemented in our minds spoken or unspoken rules about "the way things are." *I'm too old to make a change if I didn't do it years ago. I'm too young. I'm too early. I'm too late. What I want doesn't exist. I'm not allowed. This isn't how things work.* Without thinking, we have unexamined rules about the supposed way things work. These rules create and maintain a bias for limitation. When you notice a rule you've told yourself about what is or isn't possible, learn to question where it came from. At times, these assumptions are nothing more than stories you've told yourself that are in desperate need of editing.

Expansion is the perfect time to take a closer look at the limitations we have around ourselves so that we might discover how to interact with our desires with more imagination. I'm not saying that you need to pretend that limits aren't real, but I hope that you'll activate your inner skeptic toward them.

An Imagination for Abundance

We can choose to fill our imagination with limits, but we'll need more than that if we want to experience possibilities and desires expansively. If you want an imagination that can take you somewhere besides the same grocery store you go to every week, you need to learn how to feed your imagination with something more. We need to be attuned to wonder and abundance if we are to find the good that is waiting for us. Imaginations that are steeped in abundance create the oxygen needed for the sparks of desires in our lives to grow. Without oxygen, the sparks will die out too soon.

The concept of abundance can be tricky at times because we see so many negative examples of greed, opulence, and affluence that are destructive. But true abundance isn't any of those things. Abundance can include material wealth or possessions, but it also means living in gratitude, reciprocity, and mutuality with the world we live in. As Robin Wall Kimmerer reminds us in her book *Braiding Sweetgrass*, abundance doesn't have to be extractive and can happen as a result of a collective, sustainable reality given to us in respectful acknowledgment of creation.[1] Abundance doesn't come from having dominance over everything in our lives. Instead, welcoming abundance in your life is learning how to relate to your desires with openness and curiosity, even when you know you don't control others or outcomes.

Our potential to believe in goodness rather than scarcity isn't static, nor does it exist passively in us. Believing in abundance is something we have the opportunity to participate in building and helps us be better able to look for what we want and need. We actively grow this capacity in our lives through honesty, embracing the stories of others, and reexamining our relationship with uncertainty.

An Abundance of Honesty

Limitation: Being honest about what you want accomplishes nothing.

Abundance: Being honest about what you want is a chance to embody courage.

The voice of limitation says that being honest about what you want doesn't matter, so why bother? When you have this mindset, honesty is an unnecessary bother or a frightening complication to our lives to avoid because it leads to the vulnerability of being let down or disappointed. It can feel easier to live at arm's length from our desires and not admit, even to ourselves, that we long for something beyond the familiarity of limitations.

Instead, abundance sees honesty as a vital starting point and expects to be changed by it. When we are radically truthful about our desires, it's an act of courage that changes us and expands our capacity for receiving goodness. When we approach our desires as authentically as possible, it teaches us how to be brave, setting the path for the rest of our journey. What would happen if you were utterly candid about your desires, and you didn't censor yourself? What if you could be open about your genuine desires without labeling them as frivolous, unworthy, unimportant, or impossible? I know this can be scary, but I think you'll also find it to be an act of courage that changes you.

I recently found an old, half-used planner of mine on my bookshelf that reminded me of what it feels like to engage with this process of honesty and courage. When I took the planner off the shelf, I noticed it was the one I kept during the season of my life when I was just starting to look ahead after the VP job rejection. Among the scribbled notes about phone calls, appointments, and Little League games, one page caught my attention.

In this particular planner, there was a page to write down what you want, without restriction or limitation, according to four different time frames (three months, one year, three years, and a lifetime). The idea is to get in touch with your desires very honestly, and to do so for a specific scope of time to make your thinking more concrete. Under the section for the next three months, I wrote down that I wanted more comfortable and beautiful spaces in my home. (This had to do with my realizing that we needed a new couch in our family room.) I also wrote that I wanted distance and perspective, which I believe was a vague reference to the fact that I was still in a bit of a depression spiral. For the one-year period, I said I wanted to gain clarity for the next decade of my life. I also wrote that I wanted to have an approved book proposal, which is funny because I had little idea of what that would mean, how I was going to pull that off, or what I even wanted to write about. For the three-year mark, I wrote that I wanted to own a business, and for the lifetime category, I said I wanted to do meaningful work, love my family and friends well, play, and experience joy in my life.

I had forgotten that I'd written these desires down, but finding the journal again reminded me of what it felt like to name things I wanted that felt audacious and hard to attain. I didn't know how to go about any of it. I didn't know if they would ever materialize into something more than some words scrawled on the page. But I did know I was as honest as I could be.

I didn't know then that much of what I wrote down would actually happen. I got an approved book proposal. It just took three years longer than the time frame I'd written down. I made the change to start working for myself in my business full-time three years later, almost to the day, from when I first wrote it on the page. When I saw how those things had unfolded, it was uncanny and moving to realize that these desires, which were so painfully honest that it felt like a risk to put them to paper, had happened in such tangible, undeniable, and life-giving ways.

While I don't think that merely writing those words down magically made them come true, I do think that unfiltered honesty about what I wanted, without assurance that it could ever happen, was no small thing. It helped me become someone who interacted with possibilities with courage instead of limitation. Writing down my desires was a small but important part in the process of learning not to erase those desires. I don't necessarily think a blank page in a journal has the power to change your life, but I think the honesty that you fill it with just might.

Being completely up-front about our desires can be hard, but when we are transparent about what we want, we infuse our imagination with the reality of abundance and open ourselves up to see where that will take us. To be honest is to build a deeper connection to abundance in our souls. Even though it can be scary, and I can relate, let your honesty be a courageous confrontation of the limits you have placed on what you want.

The Abundance in Our Collective Stories

Limitation: Goodness for others comes at your expense.

Abundance: Goodness for others shows you what's possible.

The voice of limitation says that life is a zero-sum game. If another person experiences something good, that means there is less for you. This mindset of scarcity and individualism sees abundance for others as disconnected from us at best or a threat to us at worst. Such a limited worldview doesn't allow you to see others' stories as anything but a loss, and someone else's joy as proof that it could never happen for you. That's not how we were meant to live.

When other people experience goodness in their lives, I believe it shows you more about what is possible in yours. It opens your eyes to possibilities and proves that what you want can exist because another person's story is eyewitness evidence. It's the universe's way of saying, "Hey, do you see this? Abundance is real. Look at what could be possible for you too!"

We can choose a collective outlook that sees the presence of goodness in someone else's story as deeply encouraging and hope-producing. If we can do this, we're able to access real, living examples of abundance. When others experience good, there isn't less for you. It does not pose a threat. It poses a question about whether you have an imagination big enough to hold what you really want. If we truly embrace the stories of others, it teaches us to have more hope in the abundance that's possible in our lives too. From this perspective, jealousy of someone else can simply make us aware of our beliefs about what's possible, even though we tend to paint jealousy solely in a negative light.

Our collective stories are a gift to us and our capacity for abundance. If we can learn to receive them expansively, they enlarge our imaginations and point us away from old limitations we have placed on our desires.

The Abundance Despite Uncertainty

Limitation: You can't experience abundance without certainty.

Abundance: You *can* experience abundance without certainty. Certainty is not a prerequisite for abundance.

We tend to think of uncertainty as a bad thing because the voice of limitation says that certainty is a requirement of abundance. With this mindset, we're uncomfortable with not knowing what will happen, and we don't have much tolerance for that state of ambiguity. We often talk about pain tolerance, but we also need to consider how much uncertainty we can tolerate, because if it's not very high, we won't be able to stay in the process with our desires the way we need to. Uncertainty tolerance is part of the process of expanding our relationship to abundance in our lives.

Abundance doesn't exist because of certainty or because we always know how outcomes will unfold. It exists because it is in the nature of the divine and of the natural world that we are a part of. Nature imparts abundance to us in its wisdom. When I go on a hike, hear the birds singing, and see the wildflowers in bloom, I witness abundance that doesn't come from certainty but is at work nonetheless.

Our desires don't come with guarantees attached to them. I suspect this is a chief reason why wanting is so good for us. Our desires teach us to live with unclear and unpredictable circumstances, knowing that sometimes a lack of certainty is a good thing. Abundance can find its way to us, even when we're faced with uncertainty.

I'm reminded of an experience I had a few years ago, when I had a speaking engagement in Seattle and decided to tack on an extra couple of nights to see one of my closest friends since she lives in the area. I had finished up with work and was standing on the curb with my suitcase. My friend Jenny was minutes away from picking me up when all our plans fell through, as the lady who owned the Airbnb we'd booked decided to cancel our reservation at the last minute. Everything we'd planned was suddenly no longer an option, and we had no idea what to do instead. As we were trying to regroup, Jenny's husband, Scott, graciously offered to look for an alternate place for us to stay while we grabbed dinner, but when we set off to find a place to eat, we came across a huge line of people winding into the front doors of the 5th Avenue Theatre, a well-known and beloved theater in the downtown Seattle area.

Jenny turned to me smiling and asked if I wanted to try our luck at scoring discount rush tickets for last-minute patrons. Sometimes being canceled on and having nowhere to go can be a prime opportunity, and as luck would have it, we not only scored two tickets for the great price of thirty-five dollars each, but also managed to get seated in some of the best seats in the house. In the urgency of trying to find our assigned seats as the show was about to start, we struggled to match the letters and numbers on our tickets with the appropriate rows and sections. The kind, elderly usher didn't seem to know either. So, when the lights started to dim and a mild panic rose in me, she motioned for us to take the closest empty seats, which were in the front row, stage right.

The name of the show was *Come from Away*, and it shares the real-life story of the town of Gander, Newfoundland, when it was taken over by thirty-eight aircraft carrying 6,579 passengers after the planes were grounded and prevented from landing in New York following the 9/11 attacks. The show introduces you to the stranded travelers, the crew, and the townspeople who made meals, donated essentials, and cared for the unexpected guests. It paints a picture of hospitality, community, and uncommon kindness—the best of who we are as humans—which felt like a salve for the endless news cycles of violence and harm we see too often. The performances, the music, and the story were moving, beautiful, and healing, and after the final curtain, I exhaled slowly with tears still in my eyes and said, "Wow, I didn't know how much I needed that."

After the show, Jenny and I marveled at the fact that if we had been just minutes earlier or later, things wouldn't have turned out the way they did. Too soon, and we probably would've found our actual seats, which were sure to be closer to the back of the theater than the front. Too late, and we would've missed the show completely. Due to absolutely nothing we could control, it had all been perfectly timed.

As the night continued to unfold, Scott told us that he'd found a house through a friend who was happy to have us stay free of charge, and we felt grateful to receive that generosity. The next day, we explored the town we were staying in, rested, and talked as you do with a good friend that you haven't seen in person for over a year.

I learned something important from that experience. It convinced me that abundance doesn't need certainty to exist. The curveballs overturned all our plans, and nothing worked out the way we thought it would, and yet we were seen and taken care of. Though we faced unexpected uncertainty, the night had been perfectly orchestrated with a tenor of profound abundance. It taught me that uncertainty doesn't have to be all bad. At its best, uncertainty can show us how to live with expectation and openness, and that control only gets us so far. I don't need ironclad certainty about how my desires will work out. I need to know that uncertainty can be an abundant place. In fact, it's the kind of place I want to live in.

What if we truly lived like this? What if we believed that exerting control isn't a prerequisite to abundance? How would that change us as individuals? As a society? I truly wonder what that would do to our imagination and praxis. In a world that tells us that the only way to be seen and taken care of is to wield control and dominance over others and the planet, maybe it's revolutionary to accept that uncertainty provides its own healing and beauty. We can't eliminate uncertainty, and we have to learn to live with it, but maybe that's actually good news. When we create open, expansive space for our desires despite uncertainty, we take a step toward embracing that goodness.

A Blank Page

Imagine someone sitting across from you and holding a piece of paper, but you can't see what's on it. They tell you that this piece of paper contains possibilities for you and what you want, and you're naturally curious. They hand it to you, inviting you to take a look for yourself. When you take the paper in your hand and turn it over, you realize it's blank. Completely and totally blank. You're informed that this is by design to allow you to fill it in with whatever you want.

This isn't how we tend to live. Instead, we create boxes to check. We fill pages to overflowing with limitations, pressures, and reasonings that crowd out our desires. We put limitations on ourselves and what we want, repeating them like a kid at a chalkboard writing lines. It's not too often that we give ourselves a blank page for possibilities, to clear out space for what could be.

Just for a little while, maybe it could be worthwhile to practice filling the blank page with your most honest and courageous wants. To sit with the space of dreams and possibilities, rather than limits and restrictions. What if you let your imagination run a little wild?

[REFLECTION PROMPT]

One Hundred Desires

The instructions for this prompt are simple: Write down one hundred desires. You don't have to put any other parameters on what you write down. Nothing is too big, too small, or off-limits. Feel free to write down anything that comes to mind about what you want, even if it seems trivial, unattainable, or silly.

I originally came across the essence of this idea in a book on time management and navigating one's career, by career expert Laura Vanderkam.[2] The exercise was so interesting that after I did it, I told all my friends to do it too. Years later, when I started coaching, I recommended a simplified version for my clients to work on during this stage of expansion. It's one of my favorite prompts because it reveals so much about our imagination for possibilities, and it's always fascinating to see the unique answers that people give.

In case you want some inspiration to get you started, here are some of the things that people have included in their lists: *I want to learn to ride a skateboard. I want to see greater racial justice in our country. I want to be a present and loving parent to my child. I want to be a contestant on* Survivor. *I want to write a children's book. I want to get new running shoes. I want to create places of beauty and connection. I want to start my own business. I want to lead a team. I want to eat more tacos. I want to get out of debt. I want to reach the C-suite of my company. I want to make more money than I'm making now. I want to do something creative with my hands. I want to play more basketball. I want to plant an herb garden. I want a new job.* The possibilities are specific, personal, and infinite.

It's okay to write something down even if you aren't 100 percent sure of something. Nobody is going to tattoo this list on your body. You're allowed to change it anytime you choose. You're also not committing to putting all these things into action right now, which would probably be overwhelming. Instead, the point is to take an open inventory of everything you want, and you may even be surprised by what you find.

The point of the number, one hundred, is to keep you from overthinking what you're writing down because you don't have to edit yourself or cross some things out to make room for others. The number itself isn't magical, so if you can only get to twenty-five or thirty, as has been the case for some of my clients, that's totally fine. The point is to be honest and curious, more than getting to a specific number.

Step One: Write down one hundred desires.

1.   12.

2.   13.

3.   14.

4.   15.

5.   16.

6.   17.

7.   18.

8.   19.

9.   20.

10.   21.

11.   22.

23. _____   40. _____

24. _____   41. _____

25. _____   42. _____

26. _____   43. _____

27. _____   44. _____

28. _____   45. _____

29. _____   46. _____

30. _____   47. _____

31. _____   48. _____

32. _____   49. _____

33. _____   50. _____

34. _____   51. _____

35. _____   52. _____

36. _____   53. _____

37. _____   54. _____

38. _____   55. _____

39. _____   56. _____

57. _____

58. _____

59. _____

60. _____

61. _____

62. _____

63. _____

64. _____

65. _____

66. _____

67. _____

68. _____

69. _____

70. _____

71. _____

72. _____

73. _____

74. _____

75. _____

76. _____

77. _____

78. _____

79. _____

80. _____

81. _____

82. _____

83. _____

84. _____

85. _____

86. _____

87. _____

88. _____

89. _____

90. _____

91. _____   96. _____

92. _____   97. _____

93. _____   98. _____

94. _____   99. _____

95. _____   100. _____

Step Two: Reflect on what you discovered.

Notice what it was like to do the exercise.

How was the experience? Was it easy or hard to do?

Why do you think that's the case?

What does this show you, if anything, about how you tend to relate to possibilities and desires?

Note anything that was particularly surprising.

Was there anything on your list that surprised you?

Was there something missing from your list that's noteworthy? For example, sometimes my clients are surprised that an area of their life such as their career is a lot less present than they would have guessed, and that gives them something to reflect on.

Step Three: Group similar desires into categories.

What are the overall themes?

Some people find it helpful to notice natural groupings and organize the desires accordingly. Some categories that you could use are community, legacy and impact, family, friendships, finances, fun and hobbies, home, passions, learning, work and career, physical and mental well-being, travel, and miscellaneous.

Step Four: Identify sparks.

Which desires have an extra spark to them? Write them down and circle the ones that feel the most exciting, interesting, or compelling in order to come back to them later.

Now that you've created this honest inventory of the desires that are currently showing up in your life, you have a great starting place for the next stage. You're ready to take your desires into experimentation.

6

Stage Three: Experimentation

*The Clarity Paradox, R&D,
and Designing Better Experiments*

Michelle, a busy working mom, had recently finished an extended leave from work. During this time, she had the chance to rest deeply and take a break from her role as a thoughtful, engaged manager of her team. As she prepared to return, she started to feel like it was time for a new role. She was ready for something new, but exactly what that was, she couldn't say.

Michelle knew where she thrived and where she didn't. She had done work to embody and honor her desires and was reflective about leaving an organization she'd been a part of for a long time. We also discussed new opportunities that were starting to emerge.

We met one morning over Zoom, as she was in her car waiting to pick up her kids from school. She immediately began describing the desire fog she was feeling. "I don't know what I'm walking back into, and I don't know how to think about these new options. Everything feels fuzzy. I don't have any clarity at all."

I nodded. "That makes sense," I started. "But that's not quite what I hear. As I listen to you, I hear a lot of inner clarity. You know who you are, where you thrive, what you want, and what you don't want. You also sound certain that a chapter is ending, and you're ready for something new. Those internal realities are all very significant. Maybe you don't have a lot of outer clarity about specific situations, opportunities, and the form it's all supposed to take, but you have a ton of inner clarity."

Her eyes lit up. "I never thought of it that way, but that sounds right." She realized she had been focused on the outer clarity she lacked. But after reconsidering, she saw the wealth of inner clarity she possessed. Michelle had done a great job with calibration and expansion. She was ready for the experimentation stage.

In experimentation, you get to take your broad, beautiful, and too-big list of desires, and you narrow it down to the ones with the most natural interest and momentum to see what truly fits or not. This is important to gather real-life feedback about what you truly want. In experimentation, we answer the question, *How do you turn curiosity into clarity?*

Cultivating an Experimental Mindset

In this stage, people tend to make a mistake that I see over and over. That mistake is that they assume they have to know exactly what they want before they can move forward. They take it for granted that knowing what you want comes first, and then action comes second. "Once I know what I want, I can take a step." They also think the inverse is true. "If I *don't* know what I want, I *can't* move forward." With this mentality, it's easy to get stuck, without action or momentum.

This begins with a primary false assumption. You might not have spotted the fallacy yet because it is so common.

"Clarity leads to action."

I understand this way of thinking because this is what most of us have been taught. It's logical and linear. Step one: Know what you want. Step two: Do what you want. The flawed if/then assumption from this way of thinking says, "If I have clarity, then I can act." Then the subsequent attitude says, "Therefore, if I do not have clarity, I cannot act." Believe me, I get the appeal, and yes, it's true this happens sometimes. But it doesn't always work, and here's why.

This presumption fails to recognize that desires don't live in the head. Knowing what you want isn't meant to be abstract, conceptual, or cerebral. Desires are personal, organic, and, because of that, a bit wild. More often than not, our desires speak in the gut, the heart, the soul, and through intuition. Most importantly, desires must be embodied. Figuring out what truly fits you is not a thinking question. It's a doing question. If this is a struggle for you, you might be getting stuck trying to think your way through questions that can't give you satisfying answers solely by contemplation. A lot of the questions we tend to ask about our desires aren't great only as thinking questions. For example, these questions can sound like:

- Do I want to stay in my role as an individual contributor, or do I want to become a manager who leads a team?

139

- Do I want to volunteer my time with this nonprofit that I believe in or with another one I believe in for different reasons?
- Do I want a career in the field that I am currently in or another field that I have always wondered about?
- Do I want to push for a big promotion at work, or do I want to give more focus and attention to nonwork priorities in my life, such as family and hobbies?
- Do I want to make a significant shift to start over in a new city and move closer to my family, or do I want to put down roots where I am?

Signs that you're thinking your way through a doing question include:

- Going back and forth between two or more options without much progress
- A lot of debating between pros and cons, but not knowing which variables to prioritize (Hint: not all factors can or should be weighted the same)
- Feeling caught in a cyclical argument with yourself that makes you feel stalled and unable to move forward
- Questions that start with "Do I *really* want . . ."
- Asking "what-if" questions that leave you feeling immobilized
- Imagining future scenarios but not being able to tell whether you'd love them or hate them
- Knowing that you're probably overthinking things but not having an idea of what to do instead

A surefire sign you're getting stuck in this trap is when you make pros and cons lists, but you feel like the only thing it's accomplishing is creating a tedious ping-pong-style argument with yourself, going back and forth with no end. It's exhausting and not very helpful.

"I think I want a new challenge at work. Lately, I'm not sure how much I'm learning in this role."

"Yeah, but if I make a move, I might not want the extra responsibility. What if it feels like a burden and stresses me out? I'm already tired. Do I really want to add more? At least I know what I'm in for if I stay."

"But if I don't go for it now, I might miss out and not get an opportunity like it for a while. Or ever. I might be bored if I don't take on something new."

"And if I do, I might hate it even more, and I won't know how to get out of it."

And on and on.

If you've experienced this kind of mental seesawing, you know that it can go on for hours, weeks, months, or more. Don't get me wrong. I am a huge fan of personal reflection. But some of the questions keeping you caught are simply not the ones you can figure out by doing more and more deliberation.

Most of us believe and have been taught:

Clarity leads to action.

But I invite you to consider the following alternative:

Action leads to clarity.

This is the clarity paradox at work. We've been taught that we need clarity before we can act, but the clarity that counts is the kind that comes from action. When you're feeling stuck, action should come first. This is what will generate meaningful clarity. It may feel counterintuitive, but taking action is what will help you get clear on what you truly want. Action, experimentation, and learning by doing are your best allies when you're seeking alignment.

This doesn't mean you need to exhaust yourself by going in a million different directions. I'm not proposing a scattershot approach, which is why this stage isn't the one we start with. Just as you wouldn't buy a car without test-driving it, you also wouldn't attempt to test-drive every car on the market, which would be far too time-consuming and overwhelming. That's why we began with calibration and expansion. These earlier stages help you gather crucial self-awareness that will allow you to create experiments and take action from the basis of that self-reflection, giving you action steps with a higher probability of being right for you. We're going for educated action because thinking is great, but it's just no replacement for action.

Thinking helps you . . .	Action helps you . . .
Design better experiments	Design better alignment
Gain meaningful insight about yourself, especially your unique strengths and genius	Invest more in your unique strengths and genius to see them grow
Form solid hypotheses	Verify or disprove hypotheses with real-life data

Thinking helps you . . .	Action helps you . . .
Interpret and learn from past experiences	Apply insight from your past experiences to your present and future
Eliminate options that aren't worth your time	Create options that fit your true desires

When you have learned how to create experiments that test what you truly want, you're able to find clarity that comes from a deeper place; it is embodied rather than merely theoretical. In other words, you know what you want because you find yourself dancing down hallways.

Usually, when people get stuck, their instincts say, "Okay, you're confused. You need more time to think. Keep trying to figure it out. Really try to get the answer straight in your brain. Don't do anything until you know." If that has worked for you and eventually you come to clarity, that's great. But for some of the desires in our lives, that may never help. So, if you feel like you're stuck in an endless loop, notice the clarity paradox at work, and ask yourself if it might be time to switch your approach.

Here's an alternative. Let's call you a researcher in a lab. You are now director of R&D (research and development) of your true desires. Labs are where you test your theories and learn from the results. You find out where your hypotheses are accurate and, just as importantly, where they are not.

In this approach, "Do you want option A or option B?" is not a question answered by sitting down to think about it. It's answered in the lab of your life with thoughtful experimentation. This leads to clarity that is deep and embodied. This leads to alignment.

Principles of Experiment Design

Designing an experiment or series of experiments to test your hypotheses is an exercise in blending strategy with creativity. This process invites you to be thoughtful about how you design your experiments, why you're doing them, and what you're looking for.

Here are some principles of experiment design that will help you create clarity.

Principle One: Have a bias for action.

Prioritize actionable next steps. This is a fundamental principle of design thinking, which is a framework that teaches designers to identify the problem, ideate, and then create a prototype to test those ideas and solutions.[1] Note that action is essential but doesn't have to be overwhelming. Micro-progress is the idea of breaking something down into the smallest possible units of action to build momentum. No step is too small. It's more important to take action than to make it big or dramatic. Shrink the experiment as much as you need to keep going. Above all else, shoot for what feels doable.

Principle Two: Choose the appropriate level of risk for you.

Sometimes people get scared, thinking that putting their desires into action means completely upending their lives. Their first frame of reference is a level of change that is drastic and life-altering.

James had that kind of story. He was a driver who picked me up at the airport after a work trip. I'm not that chatty in rideshare situations, usually preferring to take in some rare moments of quiet, but James was friendly and easy to talk to. He told me he was an aspiring musician but hadn't always been. He'd had a successful and lucrative career that had slowly been killing him. In response, James sold his house, quit his job, and moved from Chicago to Los Angeles to pursue a career in the entertainment industry. His family was so concerned that they staged an intervention.

After several years of investing in his dream, he had a significant breakthrough in his career after a chance meeting that opened the right door. We had a great conversation about knowing what you want, following what makes you feel alive, and how the universe shows up when you do.

I love this story. How could you not? James risked so much to pursue his dream, and here he was, finding his way toward making it happen. Even though I'd only known him for about as long as it takes to get from the airport to my house, it made my day to hear his story, and I was genuinely happy for him. Why am I telling you all this? I say this to highlight the fact that James's story is the kind of story people think of when they imagine putting their desires into action. It's a dramatic story of making some of the biggest changes a person could make—quitting, moving, and starting over from a blank slate. Don't get me wrong—it's a great story. But if you're not in a place where you feel like you can do what James did, that is valid too. The mistake I see people make is that they think that if they can't (or won't) quit their job or move across the country, then they cannot do anything.

Action is essential. Taking the most extreme, disruptive, or drastic action is not. You get to choose the level of risk you are comfortable with, and what makes sense for you and your life.

This is the analogy I share with clients to explain this further. When you meet with a financial planner, one of the first questions they'll ask you is, "What level of risk are you comfortable with?" They will explain the distinction between low-, moderate-, and high-risk investments. They'll often describe scenarios that best fit those levels and the average expected return for each. They will also ask you to factor in your circumstances, such as age and stage of life, your financial goals, and whether you're planning for major life events like retirement, paying for college, or supporting aging parents. Based on that information, their job is to recommend the right investments with the appropriate level of risk for you.

In the same way, you get to choose the level of risk for your experiments. James chose the high-risk option when he decided to sell his house and move, leaving behind a well-paying job and starting over in a brand-new city. Though you might admire James's courage, it doesn't mean that has to work for you. High-risk investments aren't appropriate for every potential investor.

It's more important to be intentional about the level you're choosing and why. In fact, a major benefit of low- or moderate-risk experiments is that they can prevent a costly loss of time or money, like spending tens of thousands of dollars on getting a degree that has nothing to do with what you really want.

There is no one-size-fits-all approach for you or your goals. Family obligations, financial realities, your personal preferences, and other constraints are important factors to consider, and it does us no good to pretend otherwise. Maybe you simply hate the idea of taking the high-risk road and know that it won't work for your temperament. The important thing to remember is learning that you can invest *something*, even if it's the life equivalent of $50 rather than $50,000.

To give you more ideas about what this could look like, here are some more examples.

Examples of Low-Risk Experiments

(*An experiment that requires a minimal investment of time, energy, or money*)

- Have a thirty-minute informational interview with a person who has experience with an option you're considering. (Make sure to honor their time by preparing thoughtful questions.)
- Create a one-time project for yourself in an area of interest.
- Read a book on a subject you're curious about.
- Do a focused internet search to learn more about the field you're considering. For example, you can look at job postings and keep a spreadsheet to track what you find.
- Research schools or programs you're considering or talk to someone who went there.
- Volunteer your time in an area that is meaningful to you.

- Start a business that has little to no up-front investment, e.g., a service-based business with no expensive inventory or big purchases necessary.

Examples of Moderate-Risk Experiments

(*An experiment that requires a moderate investment of time, energy, or money*)

- Enroll in a certification program.
- Do a series of informational interviews. (I once did twenty of these to figure out if I wanted to accept a job offer.)
- Change jobs in your current company or organization.
- Create a short- or mid-term project in an area of interest.
- Hire a coach or mentor with expertise in what you're working on.
- Sign up for a class, workshop, or retreat.
- Apply for new jobs that interest you and go on interviews.
- Use vacation or paid time off to try something you wouldn't ordinarily have time for, e.g., if you want to write, take time off to do a writing retreat.
- Start a business that has moderate yet affordable up-front investment.
- Ask your current manager to give you a mid- or long-term project that furthers your interest, e.g., ask to supervise a younger staff member or intern if you enjoy mentoring others.

Examples of High-Risk Experiments

(An experiment that requires a significant amount of time, energy, or money)

- Quit your job.
- Take extended time off without pay, such as a leave of absence or a sabbatical, to pursue an experience that you wouldn't otherwise have.
- Change your lifestyle significantly, e.g., downsize to lower your expenditures, sell a house, add roommates or housemates, or another move that drastically alters the parameters that you're working with, so you have greater financial freedom.
- Move to another part of the country to take advantage of opportunities or resources that you would not have if you were to stay in your current location.
- Move to another country, looking to find solutions for broader issues in your life, such as health care, cost of living, pace of life, etc.
- Change career fields.
- Start a business that requires a significant investment of capital, either through bootstrapping or venture capital.
- Enroll in a degree program to gain knowledge, credibility, networks, or training.
- Become self-employed as a freelancer or other type of business.

These lists aren't exhaustive. These ideas are just a starting point to illustrate how many options there could be at different levels of risk. When you give yourself the freedom to play with the risk factor that's right for you, you can create many more potential experiments and opportunities to figure out what your desires are saying to you.

Principle Three: Apply a holistic mindset.

Our society tends to promote a mindset that says, "Your job is everything, and the goal of life is having all your desires met through that job. If you can't do that, then suck it up because you're out of luck with those desires." This attitude is not constructive, not to mention the fact that it overlooks many people, like those who are unemployed, underemployed, and those who don't or cannot work outside the home. It's incredibly limiting.

Instead, it's freeing to realize that not all desires have to be met in the same place, such as a paid job. If you imagine your life as having only one bucket to put all your desires into, which also happens to be the job that pays your bills, it limits your options and puts a lot of pressure on your job to meet a range of desires that it can't. It also means you're limited by what others are willing to hire you for, which is not entirely in your control.

I find it more empowering to imagine your life holistically—including what you get paid to do and what you do for enjoyment, such as hobbies, volunteer roles, and side projects you create on your own—in order to take the pressure off a single part of your life to do it all. Considering your life holistically helps open up creativity and agency.

For example, Lisa loved interior design, and it brought her so much joy. She had a talent for making a space beautiful and inviting, but she didn't feel like it's what she wanted to do as a career. Many people in the same scenario would therefore assume that their interest was unimportant. They would tell themselves to let it go and move on, but that's not what Lisa chose to do. Rather than ignoring her desire and love of design because she didn't see it as a professional option, she decided to volunteer with a local nonprofit that served homeless families. This agency provided these families with a place to live and decorated those spaces so that people could be welcomed into a home that felt warm and hospitable. Lisa found it life-giving and energizing to use her talents in that way and for the benefit of others. Having paid work as an interior designer wasn't the only way that Lisa could act on her desires, and seeing her life holistically allowed her to find an opportunity that brought her a lot of joy.

Capitalism tells us that our value is defined by the job we get paid to do, but your worth as a person doesn't come from the dollar value of a paycheck. The joy, meaning, and purpose you derive from something personal is not less valid than paid employment. You're a whole person with many different facets, each of which is a part of your true self.

Thinking about your life holistically allows you to be more strategic. What you do for work, the ways you connect with your family and friends, hobbies, volunteer opportunities, and so on all help you align with your desires in different ways if you know how to think about them. Not every desire can or should be met by an employer. If we embrace the holistic nature of our lives, we increase our ability to create space for our desires and design meaningful ways to put them into action accordingly.

Principle Four: Create a multi-track experiment map.

Similarly, part of what gets people stuck in knowing what they want is that they imagine clarity as focusing on one sole option. However, the quality of our decisions is much better when we don't just think in terms of yes or no and consider multiple options side by side. Using a multi-track approach keeps you from getting stuck by the pressure to decide on only one way forward before you have enough information to do so and makes your thinking stronger so you can develop several ideas side by side.

In the reflection prompt for this chapter, we're going to build a mind map of your experiments in this multi-track way. Rather than asking you to create a plan around a single potential option, I'm going to invite you to create a map that holds multiple options together. This allows you to maximize curiosity and creativity with your options.

There are four types of experiments that I usually recommend considering. If you're in a bigger life transition, such as a career change, I would suggest trying one of each type of experiment, but it certainly isn't a requirement, and you can try more than one of any type depending on the options you're weighing. On the next page is a map of the four types of experiments.

Experiment Type One: Improvement Experiment

This type of experiment seeks to improve your current situation and make it better. For example, if you're thinking about your career, this could mean figuring out how to make your current job fit you better. Your peak and contrast experiences will give you a lot of good clues about what this could look like. You can look for ways to change aspects in

```
┌─────────────────────────┐
│     EXPERIMENT MAP      │
└─────────────────────────┘
```

Wild Dream Experiment		Improvement Experiment
	Experiment Map	
New Lane Experiment		Environmental Experiment

your current role to make them look more like your peak experiences. Conversely, you can also find ways to minimize or eliminate the things that echo your contrast experiences.

For example, if your peak experiences show you that you love to develop others, you can ask your manager if there are opportunities to help train new hires or interns. Or, if you're tasked with working with a client who is particularly difficult for you but you have a teammate who has a much easier time connecting with them, you might consider proposing a shift of assignments. If you're a stay-at-home parent, you could experiment with ways to improve the way you manage that, such as looking for regular ways to interact with other parents or blocking out a certain part of the week for something that is life-giving, like a restorative practice or a project that is meaningful to you. Naturally, not everything can be changed about your current situation, so in this type of experiment, you're testing to see how much you can adjust and how those changes impact your experience of your reality. Categories of changes you could consider making are having better boundaries, shifting the responsibilities of your role or job description if you have input on that, changing who you connect with and how you spend your time, and limiting the situations that are the most draining for you.

The benefit of improvement experiments is that they build on what you're already familiar with and allow you to look for positive changes that usually add less disruption to your life. At times, improvement experiments do the trick and make a big difference in a person's experience, improving it to fit what they are looking for. Other times, improvement experiments confirm that a different option is needed.

Experiment Type Two: Environmental Experiment

This type of experiment takes what you currently do but puts it in a new environment, such as a different organization, company, type of space, or even a different department within your current organization. For example, in a work context, if you're an engineer who feels isolated as the only woman in your firm, you could start to look for female-founded firms or those with more representation. Another example might be changing departments within the same company because there's a team that you enjoy working with or that is doing work closer to your peak experiences. In a personal context, it could mean choosing to end a volunteer role that has become draining and looking for other places to invest your time.

Environmental experiments often come with greater transitions than improvement experiments because looking to alter your overall environment usually causes more disruption in your life, but they are a good way to build on some familiar elements while still branching off toward something that is new and potentially a better fit. A critical question that environmental experiments can help you answer is, Do I hate this scenario, role, or activity, or do I hate this scenario, role, or activity in this specific context?

The reason why this is important is because the environment has a significant impact on your experience of any given role. It's similar to looking for a place to live. If you're house hunting, you'll consider the house itself, such as the number of bedrooms and bathrooms you're looking for. But you'll also need to take into account the neighborhood and what the surrounding environment is like. Those are the environmental factors that you can solve for in this type of experiment.

Sometimes when people are unhappy in their current situation, they are highly affected by environmental factors but underestimate them and don't know to give them enough weight. The neighborhood you live in often matters as much as the house itself, sometimes more. This is especially important to pay attention to if you're coming out of a toxic environment. For the next season, finding the right environment might be especially critical and deserving of more consideration, even if it means taking a hit on other factors.

Also, don't assume that a negative point of reference automatically applies to all situations. Sometimes when people are processing having been in a misaligned or poor environment, they assume that all other environments will be equally bad: "No job will ever be perfect, so I might as well just stick it out with this terrible one." It's the antithesis of assuming the grass is greener on the other side. Because of a prior negative experience, the asumption is that the grass is dry and dying everywhere. No organization or situation is ever perfect, of course, but what that means in different settings, companies, or organizations is unique. And since you are also unique, how those particular weaknesses affect you will vary greatly. You're looking for a different fit, so sometimes a change in environment can be a big part of that equation.

Experiment Type Three: New Lane Experiment

These are the experiments with new paths that have crossed your mind that you don't have much previous experience with. You might have thought, "I've always wondered if I'd enjoy starting my own cookie business," or "Maybe I would like to start a career in design even though I studied anthropology in college."

Usually, when people have these wonderings, they're so different from what is true in their life now that it's a little intimidating to think about them. You're not going to become a UI/UX designer if you're currently a teacher without many other steps along the way, so it's easy to dismiss those thoughts because you see all the work involved in making a considerable shift. But, when you name the idea as an experiment, it helps you define a handful of beginning steps to help you explore without feeling pressure to have arrived.

Experiment Type Four: Wild Dream Experiment

Wild dream experiments are the desires that seem almost impossible. More than the first three types, they usually feel unrealistic. I love this category and strongly recommend creating at least one wild dream experiment as a part of your map because they are a powerful way to uncover significant desires that might be hiding away. Wild dreams deserve to be honored and can have a lot to say about what you truly want.

People have told me about wanting to travel the world, start and run an animal sanctuary, live in meaningful community, go back to school to pursue the degree that they always wanted, and many other wonderful aspirations. My advice is never to rule these out because, once upon a time, my wild dream was running my own business and writing a book, and I've seen many other people's wild dreams become reality too. But even if that's not where your wild dream experiment leads you, simply reflecting on what that would be can reveal insight about what you're longing for, which can help you approach your next steps with more clarity or spark ideas worth paying attention to.

Creating an experiment map allows you to conceive of and design experiments that help you nurture curiosity into clarity. The map shows you where you might start directing action to understand your desires and take steps that will allow your life to speak to you about how your desires are meant to come alive. Remember: action leads to clarity.

No Failed Experiments

When my kids were younger, their elementary school held an annual science fair where students would create a science experiment of their choosing and present what they learned to their class. It was always fun to see what topics the kids would pick, like how fast the family dog could run compared to a human, what design of paper airplane would fly the farthest, and what would happen to plants that were watered with milk and orange juice instead of water. My friend who helped run the fair is a brilliant scientist and engineer herself, and she loved to remind the kids that an experiment that doesn't go according to plan is *not* a failure because it still teaches you so much. She helped the children realize that experiments are supposed to either prove or disprove an initial hypothesis, and both types of results are important to the process of scientific learning and discovery.

I've always loved her mindset and invite you to adopt the same one as you experiment with your desires. Some experiments that you'll try will go beautifully. They will confirm your thinking and may go even better than planned. Other experiments will not go the way you anticipated at all. They may "fail," and that is also wonderful. The beauty of the experimental process is that everything is learning. Success and failure, positive and not-so-positive results all have something to teach us. The important thing is to focus on what your experiments reveal, learn as much as you can from them, and keep going with the process. In the next stage, we'll talk even more in-depth about the outcomes of your experiments and build on their lessons. No matter the outcome, every experiment on your map has the potential to show you something crucial about what your desires are creating in your life.

Create an Experiment Map

To create your experiment map, we'll use the process of mind mapping. If you're not familiar, mind mapping is a way to organize your thinking by visually grouping ideas, thoughts, insights, or questions around a common theme. It's an organized yet creative tool to begin to design your experiments. Mind mapping allows you to visualize what you're thinking and working on, and it helps spark other creative ideas as you see and play with different thoughts and next steps. I love mind maps as a tool for generating space for possibility, curiosity, and options.

A few practical tips: The beauty of a mind map is that it can be a place for a lot of disparate thoughts, so feel free to write whatever comes to mind. You will sort them out and discern where you want to go later, but to start, let your ideas flow without feeling the need to edit too much. I like old-fashioned pen and paper for this; some studies show that this can open up different pathways in our brains. But many digital tools are available, and I utilize those too. I've used one called Coggle, and I like it a lot. And some of my clients prefer Miro. The purpose of this is to get ideas going. You're not committing to anything yet, so when in doubt, write it down. You can edit your map later.

Step One: Identify experiments.

Create a map with a rectangle for each different category of experiment that you're considering and label each type (improvement, environmental, new lane, and wild dream).

You can leave off a type of experiment that doesn't pertain to you, and you can create more than one experiment of each kind. This is meant to inspire ideas and get you started rather than make you feel boxed in, so feel free to make it work for you and your process.

Below is an example of what that could look like if someone wanted to have one improvement experiment, two environmental experiments, one new lane experiment, and two wild dream experiments. This example is primarily a

EXPERIMENT MAP EXAMPLE

Improvement Experiment

Wild Dream Experiment 1

Environmental Experiment 1

Experiment Map

Wild Dream Experiment 2

New Lane Experiment

Environmental Experiment 2

career-oriented one, but of course this process can work for either personal or professional experiments.

After you've identified the types of experiments you want to include on your map, name the specific idea you're considering for each experiment. In step two you'll come up with practical next steps to pursue, but for now simply mark the types of and draw circles for the number of experiments you'll include. On the next page is a sample of what this could look like.

In this example, the person wants to explore improving their current role, either changing departments or companies while performing a similar type of role, exploring a new field, and considering two different wild dreams of either going back to school or starting a side project that could potentially become a business.

Step Two: Brainstorm next steps.

Now, take each circle individually and ask yourself the question, What would your plan be if you were 100 percent committed to doing this? Again, you're not actually committed to anything yet, so this is still hypothetical. But challenging yourself to come up with real-life applications is a step toward making these experiments more concrete and generating as many practical ideas as you can. Three is just a starting place; you can certainly have more circles if you have more ideas.

Get specific in your hypothetical all-in plan by addressing questions like:

What tangible steps could you take to make this a reality? Think about the different ideas that come to mind.

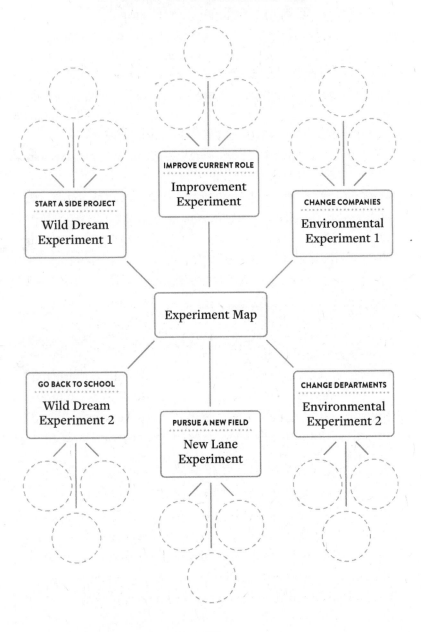

IMPROVE CURRENT ROLE
Improvement Experiment

START A SIDE PROJECT
Wild Dream Experiment 1

CHANGE COMPANIES
Environmental Experiment 1

Experiment Map

GO BACK TO SCHOOL
Wild Dream Experiment 2

PURSUE A NEW FIELD
New Lane Experiment

CHANGE DEPARTMENTS
Environmental Experiment 2

What questions do you have?

Who could you talk to in order to learn more or get connected with others?

What skills would you need to learn?

What kinds of things would you research?

The goal here is to get specific and practical to identify potential ways to get started. Let yourself be creative and put down whatever comes to mind. If you love to brainstorm, you'll love this part of the exercise. If you don't and are tempted to feel overwhelmed, that's okay. Feel free to take this as an opportunity to ask for help. You can grab a friend (especially one who loves to ideate) and invite them to help you generate possibilities and questions.

On the next page is an example of what this mind map could look like. Notice that each type of experiment has a few different possible action steps to explore what that option might look like.

Step Three: Decide which experiments to pursue.

After you've completed your experiment mind map, take a step back and notice what you have. As you look over what you've written, circle or highlight the steps where you sense the most energy and motivation. Do you have more excitement about one of these potential next steps? Conversely, are there some ideas or experiments that don't sound appealing at all? Maybe there's a whole category of experiment that sounds terrible, and you want to pin it for now.

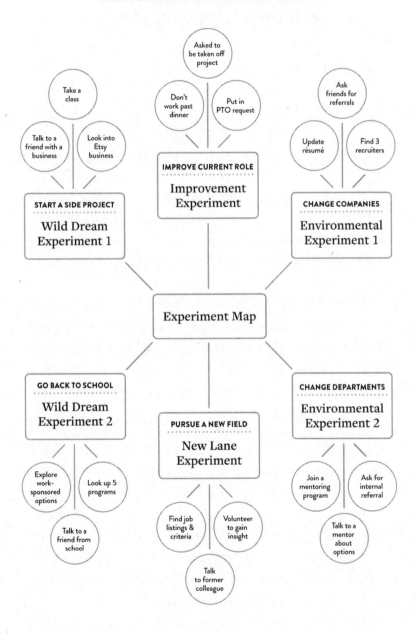

Next, this is a good time to go back to the questions that you put in your question parking lot in chapter 3. Do those questions give you other ideas of next steps to add, or change where you want to spend more time? Sometimes those questions still need to stay in the parking lot, so don't feel like you need to address all of them. However, some of the questions can inspire ideas on how to go about your experiments.

After considering your map as a whole, choose three to five actionable next steps you could try in the next month or so. (That's just a suggestion; you can do more or fewer experiments and choose a feasible time frame for you.) But remember to make the steps as small as you need them to be in order for them to be actionable. Here's an example of what this could look like at this point:

Experimentation Plan Example:

1. Improve Current Role (Improvement): Focus on setting a clearer boundary to end the workday and stop working past dinner. Notice if this changes the experience of your current role.

2. Pursue a New Field (New Lane): Talk to a former colleague. Send them a list of questions ahead of time about their experience. Ask them if they know others who might be up for a conversation.

3. Pursue a New Field (New Lane): Find job listings and create a document that tracks what kinds of criteria and qualifications might be needed.

4. Change Companies (Environmental): Update your résumé and ask five to ten people in your network if they would be willing to share it.

5. Go Back to School (Wild Dream): Look up five programs and schools that could be of interest. Write down any questions about each of them. Ask friends if they know anyone who has done these programs.

After you've completed this step, you should have a set of action steps that sound the most viable and motivating. These are the science fair experiments that you're about to run to see what happens. Always feel free to return to your map to make edits, additions, and eliminations as you continue to learn. Your map should evolve with you and your process.

In the next stage, we'll explore the outcomes of your experiments and build on what you learn from them.

7

Stage Four: Integration

*Invitations, Disappointment,
and the Goodness of Wanting*

I n my early years of coaching people through the authentic alignment pathway, the first version only had three stages and ended with experimentation. To my original thinking, the work we did in the first three stages related to calibration, expansion, and experimentation was enough. I thought that if people had done the work of those stages and knew what their next steps were, they would have everything they needed.

I learned the faultiness of this assumption when Alex reached out to me a few months after our coaching ended. When we worked together, she was in a career transition after getting burned out in her old job, and we had great conversations about calibration, expansion, and experimentation in her life. After initially being excited about what she learned about herself and what she wanted, she now felt her process was not going well, and, feeling discouraged and tempted to give up, she called me.

When we talked, and I got a chance to hear more about her experience since we'd last met, I was so glad for the opportunity to work with her and help her get unstuck; in addition, it also gave me the chance to learn that I had overlooked an essential part of the process.

Desires and reality coming together is always a new ballgame. You can plan an incredible vacation, but that's different from actually hitting the road. The good news is that you're going on your trip, but since you can never fully predict what will happen when you actually head out the door, knowing how to be adaptable, make midcourse adjustments, and respond to curveballs becomes crucial to find your way through the adventure.

It's not enough to know what experiments you want to run; you also have to understand how to read and respond to the results when things get real. You need to be able to integrate hypothesis and outcome. Understanding what happens in your experiments is essential so you can choose how you need to respond to them. A scientist who designs experiments but never learns how to interpret the results isn't going to be a very good one.

When I spoke to Alex, she filled me in on what she'd been seeing in her life. She told me that she had been engaging in several experiments and eliminated an option that wasn't right for her. She felt good about that. She was surer than ever that she needed a new chapter in her career, and all her experiments confirmed that. However, since she didn't have a job offer yet, she saw that as a sign that she was failing, and came to the conclusion that the process was going poorly. It felt discouraging.

As we talked, I listened and pointed out many examples of things that she had done that took courage and initiative, things worth celebrating, and that she had a lot to be proud of. She started to see what she had missed and said, "I thought everything was going so badly, but now I realize how many good things are happening, and I need to stick with the process. I guess I do feel kind of proud of myself." A few weeks later, she messaged me to let me know that she'd found an opportunity that was a great fit for her and she was excited to give notice and make the jump, bolstered by all the work she had done to understand what she truly wanted.

From talking to Alex and others like her, I learned how this part of the process has its own challenges because of two interrelated realities. First, outcomes are not self-interpreting. Second, bringing your desires to life depends on being able to interpret and respond well to the invitations within outcomes.

Reality One: Outcomes are not self-interpreting.

When we assume that outcomes are self-interpreting, we have a tendency to view them too simplistically—as good or bad, going well or going horribly, black or white. For Alex, she automatically thought not getting a new job meant everything was going badly. I understand why she felt that way. While it was hard not having a new job yet, integrating her desires with the real-life outcomes required much more nuance than what her first read told her. When we don't engage enough with the interpretation of the outcomes of our experiments, we're prone to misreading what the data is saying. This can cause us to miss important discoveries, give up on the process too soon, or make assumptions that aren't true, which will make it harder for us to have the resilience to bring our desires to life.

Learn to separate the outcome itself from the interpretation of that outcome. They are not the same thing. Outcomes are simply a starting point. How you make sense of what happened to you is a related but separate reality. Alex thought the only possible way to interpret not having the job offer she wanted yet was as a failure, when the reality was that she had taken many steps of growth that were beautiful, moved her forward, and were worth celebrating.

The ancient Taoist parable "Sai Weng Lost His Horse" addresses outcomes and how we interpret them. The famous story goes that a poor farmer lost a horse, and all the neighbors came around and said, "Well, that's too bad." The farmer responded, "Maybe." Shortly after, the horse returned, bringing another horse with him, and all the neighbors came around and said, "Well, that's good fortune," to which the farmer again replied, "Maybe." The next day, the farmer's son was trying to tame the new horse and fell, breaking his leg, and all the neighbors came around and said, "Well, that's too bad." I'm sure you can guess that the farmer once more replied, "Maybe." Shortly after, the emperor declared war on a neighboring nation and enacted a draft, but the farmer's son could not fight and was spared due to his injury. And once again, the farmer withheld the apparent interpretation of the events unfolding in his life. So the story goes.[1]

The point of this story isn't to be stoic as we face the outcomes of our desires and experiments, but to remember that outcomes in and of themselves are not self-interpreting. The meaning of events, in part, comes from how we see and interpret them, and sometimes our first read isn't necessarily the best one. It takes practice, skill, and nuance to be able to see outcomes with the necessary perspective to allow our desires to guide our growth.

Reality Two: Bringing our desires to life depends on being able to interpret outcomes well.

Every outcome, whether our immediate reaction is to deem it good or bad, invites us to learn, reflect, and respond in ways that help us grow, stay in the process with our desires, and ultimately create alignment. Success and failure, in the traditional sense, mean much less than knowing that the outcomes you encounter can help you take steps toward your desires and thriving.

In baseball, players read pitches to be better hitters. Their effectiveness at the plate increases significantly if they know how to identify what kind of pitch is coming their way and match their swing accordingly. On average, a player has 0.2 seconds or less to choose whether they will swing at an incoming pitch and how they will do so. The better someone can identify a pitch in that tiny interval of time, the more likely it is they'll hit well and get on base. If they misidentify a pitch or swing when they shouldn't, they will be much less successful. They might swing at pitches that weren't in the strike zone, get off-balance from an off-speed pitch, or miss opportunities to capitalize on favorable pitches.

When we understand that outcomes are not self-interpreting, but that we can learn to interpret them with intentionality and practice, it allows us to be like the hitter behind the plate with the best response to what comes our way. In the integration stage, the primary question is, How are you being invited to exercise agency with your desires? Knowing how you can engage your agency amid the unpredictable pitches coming your way is what helps you create meaningful integration between what you want and how you can bring it into reality.

Though nothing can tell you every possible outcome you'll encounter, integration teaches you to read the outcomes you'll experience and, most importantly, to see the invitations within them so you can respond in mindful ways that generate momentum within your desires. Outcomes aren't necessarily endings; they usually contain invitations to next steps and continued experimentation. Your job at this stage is to identify those invitations so you can integrate your desires with your reality.

There are five common types of invitations that I see in this stage. Being able to spot them in your life will help you learn from your experiments and make progress toward your goals. Like the batter at the plate, when you discover how to spot and respond to these invitations, you'll significantly increase your on-base percentage.

Invitation to Celebrate

When NaKhia announced that she had started her business, I was so happy for her. It was something that I'd heard her express a strong desire to do for some time, she'd been consistently taking steps toward that goal, and the time had come for her to officially launch. Within the first week, she had already booked a handful of clients and was feeling energized and excited. Truly incredible. When an outcome is a big moment like NaKhia's, it's an invitation to celebrate.

But this doesn't mean you should only wait for the most significant or dramatic times to do this. Most of us have a small target of what we consider celebration-worthy, and anything outside that doesn't register. Significant milestones are great, but they aren't the only things worth celebrating.

Instead, what if you learned how to celebrate every win? The big and the small. The times when the job offer came through, when you took your dream trip, or when you finally launched your business. But also the times when you got sincere, positive feedback from someone; took a small but tangible step toward a goal; or discovered something that brings you joy. Taking those moments to be proud of yourself honors the whole process, not just the biggest, brightest destinations.

For NaKhia, the launch was a remarkable moment. But it was just as important to celebrate the small steps of consistency earlier in the process, like keeping her journal of ideas, figuring out how she wanted to work with people, signing up for a business class, and many other instances where she experimented with her desire to be an entrepreneur. Those mattered too. When it comes to the brave work of bringing your desires to life, nothing is too small for a little celebration.

When we don't hold on to the positive and celebrate along the way, we do ourselves a disservice. When we look for progress, growth, and little ways to practice celebration and gratitude, our brains start to look for more ways that abundance is showing up in our lives. So celebrate it all. Remind yourself that nothing is too big or too small. Make a big deal of the major milestones, but don't wait until they come along to have a celebration, because the best way to get to the bigger moments is in the small steps, anyway.

If you don't know where to start, let me give you a few reasons to celebrate right now: You're here. You're asking excellent questions that some people never ask. You're taking active steps to learn how to listen to your desires, and if you understand and implement even one or two things that can be helpful and actionable, that's so important. The little things all add up.

Invitation to Keep Going

Sometimes the invitation is to keep going, be patient, and not give up prematurely on your process. This is what happens when you have strong desires, but you're not seeing the reality match them in a way that feels satisfying yet. This is what Alex was going through. She had more conviction than ever that she was ready for a new job, but it hadn't happened yet. She was working hard on applications, and there had even been one potential role that looked promising, but it didn't pan out. Rather than giving up, she learned how to see it as an invitation to keep going and to incorporate new steps.

This is especially important when you're dealing with desires and outcomes in which you have limited control. Alex could only control so much. She could network, find opportunities, and optimize her LinkedIn page, but she couldn't force potential employers to get back to her or offer her a job.

But when you're moving toward what you desire, sometimes the invitation is to keep going.

My favorite park near me is designed as a nature center with trails and community gathering spaces, and, unusual for most public parks, it uses both ornamental and edible plants in its design. Because of this, there's a variety of fruits and vegetables that guests can sample when the season allows, such as oranges, lemons, herbs of all sorts, avocados, a fig tree, and even aquaponic bok choy. In one section of the park, there's a patch of blackberry bushes. Every year, the park staff place a large sign next to the blackberries warning visitors not to mistake them for raspberries and pick them prematurely: "These are blackberries, not raspberries! Please don't pick them until they are ripe." Growth can take time—both with fruit and with our desires. If this is the invitation that you're sensing, remember that sometimes the best thing you can do is keep going.

Invitation to Engage with Disappointment

At times in our journey, we will face disappointment. I hate to say it but not all our desires will come to pass and it sucks. To compound this irritating reality, disappointment is made worse because we haven't been taught how to manage it very well. This is why living in denial of what we want sometimes seems a better option than the risk of being let down. But, when we try to avoid disappointment at all costs, we overlook the fact that it doesn't have to be the end of the story, and we can actually learn ways to stay connected with our agency amid disappointment rather than be frozen by our fear of it.

In the VP job rejection, I certainly didn't go looking for disappointment, but it was in my life in an unavoidable way. And even though it's not something I would have chosen for myself, that season taught me that disappointment isn't the enemy. It's awful but it doesn't have to have the final say.

If you learn to navigate disappointment, you'll gain a valuable skill for being able to integrate your desires with reality. If you make it a personal goal to become excellent at processing disappointment in healthy ways, you'll dramatically increase your ability to engage with this crucial part of the process. I'm not saying you have to pretend to enjoy something so painful, but if you can do disappointment well, it might just be one of your best tools in your toolbox for coming alive to your desires.

After the job rejection, a mentor gave me the best advice I've ever heard about how to handle disappointment. He had been one of the people who'd encouraged me to apply in the first place, and his support meant a lot. When I reached out to say that I was really struggling and looking for perspective on the experience, he told me to reflect on a question that surprised me.

The question he asked me was, What specifically did you want most from this role? He advised me to think about what I'd been excited about and to be as detailed as possible. This was a new train of thought—to not only consider my desire for the job itself, which I had been entirely focused on, but the precise, underlying desires that went into my eagerness for this role, what exactly I'd thought I wanted in it.

His question pressed me to think in more detail about all the excitement I'd had for the job, and I made a list of the specific things that had felt most motivating.

Here's what my list included:

1. I want something new. I want a new challenge, and it sounds weird, but I want to feel out of my depth and like I have to be forced to learn a lot and grow quickly. I'm tired of feeling bored.
2. I want a bigger scope. It feels inspiring to think on a larger scale than what I'm used to and to consider a much broader perspective.
3. I want to work alongside and invest in leaders. I want to work closely with leaders I respect who are doing great work in meaningful ways. I want to do what I can to help them grow, thrive, and feel supported.
4. I want to make more money. After being chronically underpaid, I want to be able to provide for my family. I didn't go into nonprofit work to get rich quick, but the current situation is becoming unsustainable, and we can't keep going like this.

This exercise helped me realize how the VP job might have fulfilled these desires, but that particular role wasn't the only way to receive those things. Separating the desires themselves from a single vehicle for those desires was a revolutionary idea. Clearly, the job I wanted wasn't an option, but it didn't mean all those underlying desires had to die too. I could seek out and create other ways to learn, broaden my scope, develop leaders, and increase my earnings. I could specifically look for the ways I could move ahead based on my own agency, without needing to wait for someone else to hand me the opportunity to do so. This realization was such a simple shift, but it blew my mind to see the job as one means to an end among many, many others. That gave me the needed perspective to look for other ways forward that would be equally, if not more, satisfying. A huge weight lifted from me when I realized that although the role I wanted was off the table, alignment with my deeper desires was not.

This paradigm shift framed disappointment in a new way. Disappointment wasn't the end of the story. It was a partner to my process when I focused on alignment with my desires as the true goal. As much as it hurt—almost unbearably at times—disappointment gave me a crystal clear mirror to what I really wanted. I'm the last person to minimize how painful disappointment is, but you can heal from it, and you can let it be a generative presence in your life for what you truly want. So many of us allow the fear of disappointment to cut us off from dreaming, but it doesn't have to be that way. Don't let the fear of disappointment erase your desires and who you're becoming through them.

No human has ever gotten everything they ever wanted. You probably won't be the first. Disappointment is inevitable, but it's within your power to learn how to be thoughtful about creating an approach to it that better serves you. It might sound odd to have a life goal of being really great at disappointment, but I think it would be game-changing for so many of us.

Invitation to Release What Does Not Align

Sometimes you find that you no longer want something you thought you did. Maybe the doors close and you're at peace about it. Maybe your experiments have shown you that a scenario you thought would be energizing actually drains you. Sometimes the invitation is to set down a desire that doesn't truly align. I think of the time when one of my clients thought he wanted to work in finance but, after a series of experiments, learned that it was not a good fit. There are times when you ask yourself if your desire has waned, and if the answer is yes, congratulations, you have discovered something that isn't for you. That is an important type of discovery too. You can feel great about letting it go.

A small caveat I would give is to pay attention to why you don't want it anymore. If your inner compass tells you that it's pulling you away from the you of your peak experiences, that is a very good reason. If you feel inadequate, insecure, or scared that it isn't possible or you aren't capable, that may not be a great reason, and I invite you to go back to your secondary questions and stay with the desire a little longer.

Sometimes what you learn you need to release will surprise you. This is usually a good sign because it means that you're taking risks, creating experiments, taking action, and paying attention to the results. Knowing what is not for you is as much of a gift as knowing what is for you. This type of invitation is an important part of the process. When you find yourself with the clarity to let go of something that doesn't align for you, remember that is worth celebrating too. Sometimes you have to discover what to say no to on your way to discerning what you truly want.

Invitation to Grieve

Sometimes none of these invitations apply: we come to a place where there are no ways forward or celebrations to be had. On occasion, we face outcomes that fall beyond release or disappointment. The invitation to grieve comes when what we wanted is not what we have been given and it hurts.

Hospital chaplain J.S. Park has sat with countless people as they have dealt with grief through the loss of health or the loss of loved ones. In his book *As Long as You Need: Permission to Grieve*, he says this: "Grief is the voice of what is gone. Not only the people we lose, but dreams unmade, dignity frayed, pictures with emptied frames. You can try to bury that sort of thing. I get it. I've tried it. Seems a lot easier to sever or jettison it, or shove it all into a box and force it shut. But the more you try to bury grief, the more it demands to be heard. The more you deny what the loss meant to you, the more you disappear yourself."[2] To be invited to grieve is to be invited to be present with the meaning of the loss and the fullness of everything that comes with it.

Saying goodbye to people, hopes, and desires is not easy but it is sacred, and all of us will journey through this valley at some point in our lives. If you're going through this now, I hope you are able to enter into it and know that you're not alone.

Integrating toward Alignment

In calibration, we focused on what makes you come alive. In expansion, we learned how to think beyond limits to create a sense of imagination for abundance. In experimentation, we started to build ways to generate action and clarity around potential options. In integration, we start to bring all of that together to pay attention to what truly aligns for you or not. Sometimes this happens quickly. Sometimes it takes more time. Because this work is embodied, it evolves with different seasons of your life. You're not a machine; you're a growing human being who is creating space to become someone who can hold the intensely beautiful and magical knowledge of the desires that are meant to inhabit your life.

In this stage, the most important thing is to keep paying attention to what your inner compass is saying to you. Notice which people, places, contexts, and possibilities feel like your peak experiences and which ones feel like your contrast experiences. Create genuine alignment by opening the invitations that are for you and watching what happens when you do.

It's cliché to remind you to trust the process, but I think that's because it's true. Your calibrated, expanded, tested, and integrated alignment is a beautiful whole that will continue to emerge over time. Keep going, release what isn't for you, navigate disappointment, grieve, and celebrate in each part of your life's unfolding.

◦ ◦ ◦

When I met Sam, he had enjoyed his career working in tech, but he was trying to figure out how to move forward. He'd been promoted to a team lead role, but it didn't take too long for him to discover it wasn't a good fit, and he stepped away from it because of the toll it was taking on him. Sam knew that role wasn't right for him, but he had many more questions about what it all meant. Was it all team lead roles that wouldn't work for him? Was it simply this role in particular? How much of the lack of fit was unique to the situation, and how much of it was about the way he was wired? He was asking a lot of great questions about how to interpret this experience, navigate options, and move forward.

Things became clearer as we worked through the calibration, expansion, and experimentation process. When he integrated those insights and invitations, he started to find positions that better fit everything he was learning about himself. Eventually, his experiments led to finding a new position in the same company; he was energized and motivated by a role that would challenge him to learn, giving him the opportunity to continue to develop professionally. He was excited about this shift and the team he'd get to work with and had future experiments in mind for the unanswered questions he was still thinking about.

I was thrilled to hear how the integration had created momentum in Sam's life, and his experience of the pathway stood out to me. He said, "I love this process because not only did this help me figure out why I was getting stuck and what to do about it in the present, but I also know I can return to these stages anytime I need to in the future."

I hope this pathway is one that meets you wherever you are right now, and you know you can return to it whenever you feel stuck, are at a crossroads, or encounter the new scenarios and questions awaiting you. Your ability to navigate all of the pathway will grow with you and become more refined, helping you continue to learn who you are and what you want. Meaningful alignment grows organically through the unique process that is calibrated to you, expansive in its thinking, experimental, and integrated with what your true desires are saying. As you continue on your journey, know that the wisdom you've unearthed is by your side, and there's more to come each time you need it.

Outcomes Tracker

This reflection is meant to help you process outcomes in your experiments and your process. It's designed to be done monthly to allow you to read and respond to these outcomes over time. If a month feels too often or not often enough, you can adjust the rhythm to do this more or less frequently depending on what works best for you. The important thing is to come back to this exercise on a consistent basis, building the habit of listening to the invitations and lessons from your experiments. You can use the chart on the next page, the spaces on the following pages, or a separate piece of paper to record your thoughts on.

MONTHLY OUTCOMES TRACKER

Outcome	Calibration	Invitation	Response

Outcome

Looking back on the last month, what are some of the most significant or memorable outcomes that you have seen as you have experimented with your desires? List those individually in the first column.

Calibration

Compare and contrast the outcomes you're seeing now with your peak experiences (the times when you felt most alive and energized) and contrast experiences (the times when you felt drained and depleted) that we talked about in chapter 4. You can revisit that chapter's reflection prompt if you want to refresh your memory about those experiences.

How are these current outcomes similar to or different from your peak experiences?

How are these current outcomes similar to or different from your contrast experiences?

Would you say that this outcome feels more like a peak experience, contrast experience, or a mixture of both? Why do you think that is the case?

Invitation

Based on your thoughts about how this outcome compares to peaks and contrasts in your life, what is the invitation that you sense within this outcome (e.g., celebrate, keep going, engage with disappointment, release, grieve, or something else)?

Response

What are one or two next steps you can take in response to this invitation?

Are there any ways that you feel stuck or need help and support to take this step?

Remember that integration is where your desires get lived out. It's important to stay in the process of taking steps, and even more important to stop and learn from the ways you are moving forward. Keep in mind that when you're in this stage, you're probably doing a much better job than you give yourself credit for. Be proud of yourself for any and all steps that you continue to take. No matter the outcome, you can learn to knit your desires together with the reality of your life.

PART 3

MOMENTUM, MYSTERY, and ALIGNMENT

8

The How-Tos of Desire-Based Goal Setting

We began in chapter 1 by talking about desire fog and what it feels like when you don't have a good answer to the question of what you really want. The authentic alignment pathway helps you examine your life so you can answer that question meaningfully. This process is often crucial when you're facing a significant transition, but being more deeply connected to the power of your desires doesn't have to be reserved solely for those life-altering decisions.

Even after the desire fog clears, the magic of knowing what you want can continue to give you guidance and imagination for your life. When you are able to connect what calibration, expansion, experimentation, and integration look like for you to the things that you want to see happen today, this month, or this year, you can live out the wisdom of your desires in the season you're currently in.

This brings us to a necessary conversation about goal setting. I would argue that goals and the creation and pursuit of them are an area of our lives that can benefit from seeing our desires as friends with wisdom to offer us. Truly knowing what you want should change your approach to the various types of goals that we encounter in life in dynamic and impactful ways.

There are plenty of books, articles, podcasts, tips, tricks, and general advice about goal setting, but I still feel like there is room to talk about goals, especially better practices to approach them than the traditional ways of goal setting. An example of this that most of us have had experience with is making New Year's resolutions.

Love them or hate them, most of us have tried keeping New Year's resolutions at some point in our lives but can't say that they've added up to much; we are often unchanged by them, except for perhaps being a bit more frustrated and jaded. Case in point: If you were to ask your friends about their New Year's resolutions anytime past January, what kind of reactions do you think you would get? Maybe you happen to be friends with people who love resolutions, but more often than not, you'll likely hear everyone get pretty annoyed. Discussing resolutions is like asking people to think about their goal-setting failures. The cycle is familiar. It's great when we are wide-eyed and hopeful, looking at the clean slate of a new year. But when that feeling fades, oftentimes shockingly soon, we're back to where we started, no closer to our goals, and then it's expected that we try it all again next time.

Research shows that New Year's resolutions are notoriously unsustainable and are long forgotten by February. Research suggests that only 9 percent of Americans who make resolutions complete them. I expected it to be low, but that surprised me. That means that for something still pretty universally accepted as one of the most popular practices of goal setting, 91 percent of us fail at it. According to studies, 23 percent of people quit their resolutions by the end of the first week, and 43 percent quit by the end of January.[1] There are even some unofficial dates that mark the occasion. "Ditch New Year's Resolutions Day" is January 17, and the second Friday in January is called "Quitters Day." Considering all this, it might be more amazing that we keep trying to make New Year's resolutions than the fact they inevitably fizzle out.

But suppose you're interested in intentionally building a life that helps you thrive, and your choices are either pursuing goals in a wildly ineffective way or abandoning the whole realm of goal setting altogether. Neither option sounds great, but sometimes it feels like that's all we have to work with.

That's why it's important to remember there's more than one way to create a goal, and not all goals are created equal. You're not asking for too much if you think a goal should do more than feel unattainable and weaken your morale. We typically use the word *goal* to mean a lot of different things, and we need to be more specific and thoughtful about how they do and do not work best in the real-life conditions of how we actually go about life. We also need to have better conversations about how we can approach goals with more freedom and creativity within the realities of being human with one another, rather than struggling on our own.

When goals aren't working well, most people assume it's because they lack discipline, willpower, self-control, or sheer determination. A lot of people tell me about the self-judgment they carry about their lack of discipline. People who are objectively accomplished regularly lament their failures of self-discipline. I think it's important to question where that experience comes from and why so many of us often have this idea of ourselves.

Discipline can be a word that makes a lot of us feel bad about who we are and how we do life. However, the original meaning of the Latin root of discipline, *disciplina*, is simply "to teach" or "to learn." I love this because this reminds me that goals and the discipline needed to pursue them are, at their root, a way to learn, hopefully about how to become the kind of people we want to be. Traditional approaches to goal setting often fail to help us remember this.

Grace is a working mother of two in her early fifties who regularly runs marathons, which is already extremely impressive in my book. But when she told her friends that she was thinking about signing up for the legendary Ironman Triathlon, many of them were both excited for her and blown away that she would consider taking on a goal like that.

As you may already know, the Ironman is one of the most intensive endurance athletic events you can imagine. It consists of a 2.4-mile swim and a 112-mile bike ride and concludes with a 26.2-mile, marathon-length run. The event has a seventeen-hour time limit, with cut-off times for each leg. It makes you wonder what on earth the first person who dreamed this up was thinking. "I know! Let's swim for two hours, follow up with a seven-hour bike ride, and finish with five to six hours of running." According to the World

Triathlon Corporation, there are hundreds of races like this around the world, and the Ironman motto is: *Swim 2.4 miles! Bike 112 miles! Run 26.2 miles! Brag for the rest of your life!* Indeed, people who train and push the human body to such athletic extremes have earned the right to brag their hearts out.

Grace spent over a year training for her first Ironman while raising money for clean water in developing countries. She trained on a team, spending her evenings and weekends on a training schedule split between biking, swimming, and running. It took an incredible amount of hard work and commitment to get to the starting line, especially when she didn't fit the mold of a traditional Ironman triathlete.

When I talked to Grace, she had finished her first race, and it had not gone the way she wanted; however, she was already talking about beginning to train for her next one. I was curious about what she would say about the experience. When I asked her what motivates her to compete on this level, she said, "I want to push myself to do things I didn't think possible. I want to face my fears and learn how to pursue this goal, and I enjoy the process."

To those of us on the outside, we see incredible commitment, resolve, and the things we typically associate with having a lot of discipline. But Grace described her personal experience as one of enjoyment, energy, and genuine desire. She had hard days and challenging moments, but overall, her goal to be an Ironman triathlete was one that represented a balance of challenge and motivation.

Hearing her story made me wonder if Grace was onto something that could be for all of us, even if we're not necessarily interested in signing up for the next Ironman anytime soon. What makes a challenging goal feel enjoyable? What about our traditional ideas of goal setting makes it harder for us to experience the way that Grace was living?

Traditional goal setting says that goals are first and foremost an exercise in discipline, involving individual self-control and a rigid, unchanging plan you stick to no matter what. Accomplishing that goal (or not) becomes the standard by which you are judged. If you do not reach it, you're deemed lazy. But if you do reach your goal, then you get to call yourself disciplined. This narrow framework can feel like it sets us up to fail.

On social media, I asked folks to weigh in on what the word *goals* made them think or feel. I mentioned I was getting ready to speak about goals, and I wanted to hear people's thoughts, but I didn't give much in terms of parameters for sharing. I wanted to give people open space to talk about how they experienced goals in their lives. Can you guess what was the most repeated response? It was *dread*.

When we experience dread, it's a red flag warning us something is significantly misaligned. Usually, dread happens when there is a disassociation between our internal reality—what feels true to ourselves—and the external demands being put on us. Often, this can be exacerbated by power dynamics if those external demands are being put on us by someone who also happens to be an authority figure. I remember one person telling me about their experience of working in a toxic environment and how they came to dread the mere thought of going to work. At first, they noticed the feeling of dread settling on them each Sunday night when they looked ahead to being back in the office Monday morning. Then, the weight of dread started falling on them earlier on Sunday morning, then Saturday. It got to the point where they would end a work week on Friday already dreading having to go back on Monday. It is soul-crushing to live with that kind of dread.

Responses talked about how goals can inadvertently create dread in us. People expressed the difficulty of feeling a strong misalignment between themselves and the goal-setting process.

> *I feel anxious because I feel like I will need more discipline than I have to reach the goals.*
>
> *The word* goals *feels cold and unapproachable.*
>
> *It feels like I have to be a workaholic to reach goals.*
>
> *I feel pressured to achieve goals in a way that isn't authentic to me or the way I function.*
>
> *It makes me feel like it's pushing the idea that we're not good enough.*
>
> *I feel overwhelmed and pressured.*

We don't have to create goals this way. Goals don't have to be something that we'll never attain, kill ourselves trying to reach, or abandon altogether. I propose another way. What if we envisioned holistic ways to interact with goals that took our humanity into account? I believe it would be powerful to learn to develop goals that help us become more of the kind of people we want to be and create meaningful momentum in our lives individually and collectively. Rather than settling for dread, I want to see us interact with goals that are energizing—because what if goals could feel good?

Creating Desire-Based Goals

A few years ago, when I was wrestling with what to do with the new year and already knew that the conventional New Year's resolutions wouldn't work for me, I decided to construct desire-based goals—goals that would intentionally be built on what I really wanted. I simply wrote down twenty things I wanted to see happen that year. I tried to pay attention to why I wanted to accomplish each goal in the first place. For example, one of my goals was to read twenty-five books that year because I wanted to learn from authors whose perspectives I valued. I also set a business goal for how much I wanted to make that year; it represented a big stretch for me, but it felt motivating to think about that possibility. It gave me ideas of new risks to take. I didn't reach that goal that year, but I did the following year when I put it on the list again. Other goals were less concrete and more about a quality of relationship with myself, my inner life, or my family. I noticed how enjoyable it was to come back to these goals each month, and maybe most importantly, I felt zero dread. I felt engaged, creative, and motivated by the goals I had set for myself because each of them was formed by asking myself what I really wanted in that year of life.

When I shared about that experience, people started asking questions about how to do it for themselves, so I created the three-by-five method for designing a year. It's based on simply naming three desires or intentions for the year in five categories: values, centeredness, relationships, learning, and outcomes. This method reflected the spirit of my list of twenty in that it asks you to prioritize what you sincerely want, rather than what you think you should do. People who've tried out this method have come back to tell me that they felt inspired and unrestricted by it. One person said they usually struggle with goal setting but found this method life-giving, and some of the things they set as goals were surprising. Hearing from people about how this tool has helped them reframe their process of goal setting has brought me so much joy, and, from their experiences, I've learned that when you create goals that draw on the wisdom of what you want, goals can feel uplifting, helpful, and, yes, even good.

Creating desire-based goals puts you, your desires, and your experience at the center. Goals developed this way exist to help you create action and momentum toward what you truly want. They're meant to be generative rather than a way to prove yourself. They're meant to challenge you and help you thrive, and desire-based goals tend to feel good instead of filling you with dread.

Traditional Goal Setting	Desire-Based Goal Setting
Should	Want
All discipline	A blend of desire and discipline
Desires are the enemies of goals	Desires bring goals to life
Creating and reaching goals is a linear process	Creating and reaching goals is a dynamic process
Your internal reality is irrelevant	Your internal reality is essential
Ends justify the means	Process matters

Traditional Goal Setting	Desire-Based Goal Setting
Not reaching a goal is a failure	Not reaching a goal is a chance to learn
All or nothing	Midcourse adjustment is necessary

This isn't to pretend that every goal in your life can be like this or always feel great. The reality is that there are goals in our lives that we don't author or control. This comes with being an adult. Also, sometimes a goal we have for ourselves feels absolutely terrifying, but hopefully, it's a good kind of fear. So, I'm not saying we need to pretend every single goal will always feel nothing but great all the time. But I think it's a problem if our *only* experience of goals is dread and disconnection. Engaging with goals centered on alignment, our creative selves, and our desires can be an indispensable way to reclaim the concept, creation, and pursuit of goals.

Start with listening to your desires.

This might sound basic, but I have to say it because I've been a part of so many goal-setting meetings, conversations, and discussions where nobody ever considers desires at all. While people think they are talking about goals, they're actually talking about tactics, plans, and metrics. The conversation jumps into those things, but no one has asked, "What do we want to see happen? What are the things that we desire to come from this and why?" I see this all the time, and when I ask people what their desired outcomes are, most people laugh a little sheepishly and say they haven't thought of asking that. It's easier than you'd think to start making plans and schedules before figuring out what you really want to see happen.

You've likely heard of a popular goal-setting rubric called SMART goals. SMART stands for specific, measurable, achievable, relevant, and time-bound.[2] For example, a goal of improving your health might be made more actionable by using SMART criteria, like committing to take a walk after dinner three nights a week for three months. The framework helps make your goal attainable so you know whether or not you're doing it. I appreciate how the tool helps foster clarity, but if you're not thoughtful about why you want to improve your health in the first place, why you would choose one form of movement over another, what fits you, and other desire-based considerations, I think the goals are missing something important. Do you want to manage stress, make time for movement you truly enjoy, or be able to continue to be mobile and active as you age?

Before jumping to specifics, time frames, and action steps, my favorite question to start any goal-setting process is, "What are the outcomes you're excited to see?" Naming and centering the emotion of excitement is designed to draw out desire, motivation, and where your interest and energy naturally lie. This helps you create goals in alignment with your wants. Having clarity about your desires from the start often helps to bring the particulars into better focus.

Kelly was working on her grad program, which was no small feat because she was also working full-time with many responsibilities on her plate. She wanted to set some goals around school, but when she thought about goals from a discipline-based standpoint, she quickly felt demotivated and stifled. When we talked about the question of what she was most excited to see happen, Kelly realized she wasn't chiefly motivated by the idea of getting a degree or even learning for its own sake. She was most passionate about getting to communicate and share what she was learning with a team of younger leaders she was mentoring. Having the space to think about what she truly desired gave her the ability to dream about ways to do that through pursuing this degree program. Articulating that desire-based outcome opened up goals for her time in grad school that felt much more creative and joyful. When you create goals from desires, it helps them to feel both *exciting* and *actionable*. In order for goals to be fruitful, you need both. You can start creating desire-based goals by asking this simple but often overlooked question: What am I excited to see happen?

Do a goal-setting calibration.

Another way to create goals that foster alignment is to intentionally learn from your own best way of pursuing goals. In coaching, I have a lot of opportunities to talk to people about how they are approaching goals in their lives. Whenever someone tells me they are struggling to accomplish a goal that they genuinely want to see happen, I always ask them, "Could you tell me about a time when you were able to reach a goal and also did it in a way that felt good to you?" I invite them to describe what they did and how they worked, and to notice the elements of a past experience that helped them the most.

Before we move to any thoughts about next steps or ideas of how to proceed, it is vitally important to get a clear picture of what it looks like when they are at their best with their goals. I want to help them understand when they have felt that in the past and what that previous experience might have to say about how to recreate that momentum in the present challenge. Typically, this leads to very different types of ideas, insights, and next steps, rather than merely trying to think of the "right" ways to proceed.

Hopefully, this sounds familiar to you. This is the same thinking and process we used in the calibration stage when we reflected on peak and contrast experiences. In this case, however, you're looking for clues about how you approach the area of goals that was effective, enjoyable, and attuned to your unique self. Essentially, this entails finding a goal-setting peak experience in your life so you can learn from it.

You could discover specific questions you asked that helped you unlock something important, certain types of environments that helped you most, individual ways you were supported by others, unusual practices that tapped into your approach and motivation, or other distinctive details that give you important clues to your personal style and approach to goals. When you notice what has worked for you before, you'll often find your best routes to move forward. Doing a goal-setting calibration enables you to pay attention to your unique stories and strengths and helps you leverage the best of who you are rather than ineffectively trying to replicate somebody else's methods. The way that you pursue goals should be mindfully contextualized in your life and experiences.

The reflection prompt at the end of this chapter specifically guides you through this, and it will be a great place to start.

Understand the role of desire and discipline in goals.

Lastly, understanding what goes into a goal allows you to approach it with more creativity. Most goals aren't pure discipline. They tend to be a mix of desire and discipline. Seeing the interrelationship between those things gives you insight into how to design and engage with goals in a life-giving way.

Desire gives the heart, will, and animation for a goal. It's what brings a goal to life. Discipline provides shape, structure, and consistency for goals to become a reality. Discipline and desire each play a necessary role in the process of creating and keeping goals. The goal mix diagram below describes this relationship.

High Discipline / High Desire = Inspiration

When both discipline and desire are high, you get inspiration. Inspiration happens when desire is coupled with a healthy dose of discipline. When you experience a goal like this, you'll notice higher degrees of commitment, enjoyment, and excellence that are much harder to come by when either discipline or desire is missing. I think of Grace and the Ironman. She had a strong desire for that kind of training and the routines, support, and structure to pursue the goal. But even if your desires don't lead you to high-endurance athletics, bringing together desire and well-thought-out discipline helps you work toward goals in a motivating and sustaining way.

High Discipline / Low Desire = Obligation

When discipline is high, but desire is low, you get obligation. Obligation creates goals that feel neutral at best and burdensome at worst. I think this is why most people who

responded to my question on social media described goals as an exercise in dread. They were speaking to a version of goals that was all discipline and no desire.

While it's unrealistic to think that we'll never have goals like this in our lives, it can be a warning sign if all your goals are in this category, and I invite you to reassess how you approach goals if you find that's the case. Obligation is a fact of life and can't be avoided. But what can be avoided is a life *solely* built on this type of goal.

Low Discipline / High Desire = Inclination

Low discipline with high desire creates inclination. This is the experience we have when we want something, but we don't have any habits, systems, plans, or support to see it through. We might have some desire, but we haven't created enough structure around it.

Not all inclinations have to become inspiration. For instance, when it comes to travel plans, there have been plenty of trips I've wanted to take that I never did, but it was still fun to imagine the possibilities. As someone with many ideas, I probably shouldn't aspire to have every inclination become a real-life commitment. We'll all have some things in this quadrant and that's okay. But if you notice that you have a desire you're struggling to turn into reality, it could be time to consider how discipline can contribute to your process. You don't have to go to Paris. But if you want to go, you'll need some discipline to help you get there.

Low Discipline / Low Desire = Nonstarter

Goals that are in this quadrant have neither desire nor discipline. They don't have a lot of momentum and peter out after a short time. They're nonstarters. I believe this is what New Year's resolutions are for many people when they come up with something not based on their desire but instead on what they feel like they should be doing or how they should improve. Desire is missing from the start, and they also don't create any plans, systems, habits, or support to build real momentum. So it's not that much of a surprise that these types of goals don't go very far.

When desire and discipline work together, goals take on a different feel. They're more enjoyable and positive. They're less motivated by guilt and shame, so returning to them feels like a positive, welcome experience rather than a burden.

Goals as Learning Tools

In desire-based goal setting, goals are, at their core, a way to learn about your desires and how to put them into action. They're also a chance to learn more about yourself. Ideally, they help you listen to yourself and make adjustments when necessary. Making midcourse adjustments isn't a failure; it's smart. Grit and determination are essential, but even the leading researcher on grit, Angela Duckworth, doesn't recommend keeping with goals that aren't working or fundamentally lack substantive interest or desire.[3]

More specifically, we can learn how to check in with goals in a way that helps us engage them. Usually, when people set a goal that they aren't following through on, it starts a cycle of self-judgment. They call themselves mean names like lazy and undisciplined, then try to summon more willpower to do what they said they would. It doesn't usually work out that well.

But the next time that happens and you find yourself not able to act on a goal that you made, try using this goal check-in to help you find different paths forward.

The first step is to acknowledge that you're feeling stuck, but rather than inflicting guilt or judgment on yourself,

GOAL CHECK-IN

···· **START HERE** ····

You've gotten stuck and have not reached your goal
This is neutral and a chance to learn

↓

Do you still want to?

↙   ↓

No   ## Yes
Move on without guilt   Time to get curious

↓

Assumption
You have a good reason for feeling stuck

↓

What is missing?

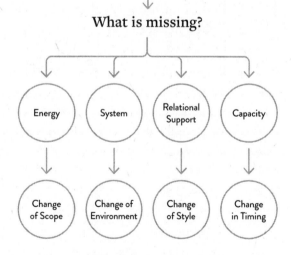

| Energy | System | Relational Support | Capacity |

↓ ↓ ↓ ↓

| Change of Scope | Change of Environment | Change of Style | Change in Timing |

What will you try next?

remember that this is a neutral piece of information. It's telling you something, but don't assume it's telling you something negative about you or your character, which is a lot of people's first reaction. Instead, hold this as a bit of objective information that gives you a chance to be curious and learn.

Next, ask yourself if the desire is still there. If the answer to that question is no, and you no longer want that goal or feel it doesn't align, that's great. This could be a chance to release something that doesn't fit you. When you learn what doesn't align for you, that's valuable insight, too, as we talked about with outcomes in chapter 7. However, if the reason why you don't want it is because of one of those tricky secondary questions, like you're wondering whether it can really happen (pragmatic questions), or you think you don't have what it takes to get there (competency questions), then I encourage you not to necessarily give up on your goal until you've done some more work with it.

If the answer to the question "Do you still want to pursue this goal?" is yes, then it's time to dig a little deeper. When you notice that you genuinely want to pursue a goal but it's just not happening, give yourself the benefit of the doubt that you probably have a good reason for getting stuck, and your task is to figure out why and what you'd like to do about it. Here are some common ways to diagnose why you might be experiencing obstacles with a goal, as well as ideas of what to do about it. These can help you decide what you want to try next and how you would like to iterate with your desire-based goal.

Missing Ingredient: Energy

If you're missing energy, consider a change of scope.

If the fundamental desire for the goal is there, but you notice a lack of energy or motivation to get started, consider a change in scope. Sometimes goals are more daunting than they need to be because we haven't played around with the scope of the goal. This is where I love to come back to the beauty of taking a micro-step, the idea of making the next step as small as needed to pull it off. This way of thinking simply invites you to shrink (and keep shrinking) the next step or two. You may not feel like you have ten weeks to take a course to learn a new skill, but you could probably find fifteen minutes to watch a YouTube video. Or ten minutes to read a single article. You can shrink a next step as small as it needs to be in order to feel doable. Consistency over time matters more than the size of the next step.

When I was learning how to build a website, I was completely overwhelmed by all the different pieces needed to pull off a project like that. The copy, the graphics, the overall layout, not to mention learning a new platform as a nontechnical person. Couple that with a ton of fear and anxiety about the process to begin with, and it was very easy to feel overwhelmed. But I knew I needed and wanted a website, so it wasn't a desire I wanted to put aside.

During that time, it helped me to think of the process as similar to taking my daily vitamin—taking one small step at a time—which might not be noticeable to anybody else but was just enough to keep me moving. I would not have been able to pull off the website by setting an intense deadline, like finishing the site in a day, but I could take one next step at a time. Write one section. Source five images. Edit one page. Even though each step felt miniscule, and it was tempting to see it as insignificant, doing that steadily over time added up. At the culmination of all those small steps, I'd managed to teach myself how to design and launch a website. But I wouldn't have been able to do it if I hadn't permitted myself to keep the scope as small and doable as possible. Motivation speaks, and if you're willing to be curious and listen to it, it will tell you a lot. When you feel stalled out, let that be a sign to revisit the scope and allow yourself to make your next move as small as it needs to be for you to feel that you can act on it.

Missing Ingredient: System

If you're missing a system, consider a change of environment.

Sometimes what you need is a better environment to engage with your goal. You have the desire, but you don't have enough support or scaffolding to help you get there. When that happens, you may not have the proper tools or setup to help you move forward. Sometimes you know what step you want to take, but your environment is making it harder for you to get there. That's when it can be beneficial to look at how you can change the system to better support progress toward your goals.

I heard an example of this when I listened to an episode of the health and wellness podcast called *Zoe*, and a doctor was describing how he keeps up a daily habit of doing strength training in his pajamas as he's making his morning coffee. This five-minute practice is simple, and because it is embedded in his routines and rituals, it means that he has created a system for reaching his goal that is doable and sustainable.[4] One of my clients wanted to do more swimming, so they joined a local gym with a pool that was next to where they worked. Another person told me about how they wanted to be more intentional with their finances, so they signed up for a budgeting service that would help them do that. There are a lot of ways to think about how to set up your environment to give you the right kind of tools, system, and structure for your goals.

Missing Ingredient: Relational Support

If you're missing relational support, consider a change of style.

As we discussed at the beginning of this chapter, beating ourselves up is easy. Many people chalk it up to a lack of discipline or character when they fall short of a goal. "I'm just so bad at following through on this." "I'm too lazy to get this done." "I don't have enough discipline." Our individualistic culture perpetuates this kind of self-talk and says that the only way forward is to try to muster up enough energy on our own. But this way of thinking overlooks how we are wired for relationships and might actually need to look for people who can support us.

This is why I'm a huge fan of helping us realize that we don't have to do it all on our own. We can explore ways to collaborate with others, such as teaming up with someone else, talking to somebody to get their opinion or expertise, or even simply coworking with someone else in person or online. This is especially important if you know that you tend to do your best work in a conversation-oriented or relational style. One of my clients talked about how hard it was for them to create a strategic plan on their own. By themselves, they would sit for hours and feel completely blank when it came to thinking about writing a plan. But they noticed that if they called someone to talk about it, they got it done, did a better job, and enjoyed it much more. Even things that we typically conceive of as solitary endeavors can be a chance to draw on relational support. So, if you notice that you're feeling stuck, some of your best ways forward may mean enlisting help from other people rather than spinning your wheels on your own.

Missing Ingredient: Capacity

If you're missing capacity, consider a change in timing.

A final category to consider is your capacity. Sometimes people tell me that they are going through an intense season that is particularly demanding, whether it involves parenting, geographic moves, caring for aging parents, grief, or any other period of life when you may have significantly diminished capacity. It's important to pay attention to that rather than pretending everything is business as usual.

If you're seeing a capacity issue, but you still want to pursue the goal that you have for yourself, try adjusting the timing of the goal. One way to do this is to lengthen the amount of time to allow for slower, steadier progress, which might make the goal less taxing. Another possible way to create a different timeline is to postpone the goal a few months into the future or a later date when you anticipate having greater capacity. When I was grieving the loss of my dad, I used both of these tactics by giving myself a longer timeline for some goals while pressing pause on others. As I moved through the grieving process and my capacity returned, I was able to come back to the goals.

Having the ability to assess where you're getting stuck in your goals allows you to continue to find the best ways forward that fit your changing, real-life circumstances.

Goals as Self-Awareness

Conventional approaches to goal setting can work to pull many people further away from themselves. People develop a mindset that puts them at odds with a goal that needs to be carried out, no matter the cost to themselves. The process is impersonal and distant from who they really are. Reimagining goals as creative, desire-based ways to discover more about ourselves can help so many of us experience goals as life-giving ways to spark our creativity, learn, and experience meaningful growth. Goals can become a way to engage with ongoing learning about some of our life's best, most interesting questions and to understand our personalized ways of approaching these goals.

What we really want should be reflected in the way we create and pursue goals. Rather than being a hollow experience, goal setting can be an opportunity to get in touch with the unique dynamics of our desires and our approach to goals. When you know your personal best ways of creating and reaching goals, you have the keys to unlock joyful self-awareness and momentum in your life.

Creating a Goal-Setting Calibration

This reflection will help you utilize the same calibration process (name, notice, categorize) that we used in chapter 4 to create an understanding of your specific approach to goals. Calibrating in this way will help you pay attention to what is most productive and satisfying to you, and drawing on your lived experience will allow you to leverage your unique style as you work toward your current and future goals. This process should feel very familiar because you have already done this with your peak and contrast experiences, and you can build on that. You can reference any peak or contrast experience you have already reflected on in the calibration stage. But I find it most helpful to pay attention to experiences that are specific to creating and keeping goals, so that might mean coming up with new scenarios for your peak and contrast experiences that will yield better reflection and insights unique to goal setting.

Step One: Name your favorite goal-setting experiences.

Recall a few of your favorite goal-setting experiences. Pay special attention to when you reached your goal, i.e., got where you wanted to go *and* felt good about the process. It's important to look for examples from your life when you accomplished a goal and did so in a way that felt grounded and true to who you are. Write down one to three experiences that come to mind. They can be recent or farther in your past, related to big or small goals, and personal or professional—whatever comes to mind.

Step Two: Notice the details of that experience.

Note what steps you took to reach that goal. Look for specifics about your approach—what you did, why it worked, and what steps you took to reach your goal. No detail is too small to notice when you're working on calibration. Did you ask a certain set of questions? How did you handle timing and time frames? Did you work on this goal alone or with other people? How did that affect your experience? Make note of any details related to how you approached, created, and implemented this goal. It's especially important to pay attention to what you found most motivating or positive about working on this goal. What made it feel enjoyable? All these details are incredible clues about the kind of goal setting that works best for you. Don't edit yourself; simply write down any details that come to mind.

Step Three: Categorize your unique approach.

Finally, start to categorize what you're finding by naming three to five keys for your best ways to create and sustain desire-based goals. Synthesize what you're learning about your goal-setting style by identifying the most helpful things that you can carry forward. Summarize what you learn about your unique approach and your best ways to work toward goals. If you utilized a personality assessment or tool like that, make any connections to those insights as well. Finish by identifying a few next steps that you can apply toward your current goal.

You can also repeat this process with a contrast experience and look for the things that tend to work against your best ways of pursuing goals, which can give you another set of related but distinct ideas about how to bring goals to life for you.

This goal-setting calibration helps you learn from the bright spots of your previous goal-setting experiences. When you have identified the unique keys to your goal-setting style and preferences, you'll be able to apply them to your current and future goals.

9

What If What You Want Actually Wants You Back?

I *think my desires are stalking me.* Allow me to explain. I've been collecting evidence over the years that makes me think something is up, but I want to give you some snapshots of moments that unfolded since that magical day at the beach, so you can tell me what you think.

Moment One

Six Months Since the Dolphin Sighting

My best friends Jenny, Erna, Jen, and I get together for a weekend trip at least once a year. If you also have best friends who live in other cities, you know how valuable this kind of thing is. This time, we're staying at a cabin on Puget Sound, and the surroundings are stunningly beautiful. The back deck opens to a view of a forest of trees that stand at the edge of the water, as if they're hoping to dip their toes in at any moment.

As the local, Jenny is playing host, and she's secured this beautiful place to stay, collected us from the airport, and stocked up on delicious food. As we're settling in, she proposes that we do a creative reflection exercise together for one of the afternoon activities.

More specifically, the plan is to depict our relationship to patriarchy by trying to capture it in a painting. If the idea of painting patriarchy makes you scratch your head and feel unsure of what that could possibly mean, then you and I share something in common because that is my immediate reaction. I am no visual artist and I'm not entirely sure what will come of this, but I'm still game to try. It seems like a chance to try something out of my comfort zone in any case. We plan to spend the afternoon painting and come back together to share and discuss what we've made in kind of an art show of our own making.

Jenny places canvases, brushes of all sizes, and a variety of paints in brightly colored tubes on the table. She's also brought scissors, glue, and a very large stack of magazines for collages to give us options. When I sit down to give it a try, I pick up the collage materials because they seem like a better fit for my well-meaning but not-that-existent artistic abilities. I pick up the magazines and start flipping through the glossy pages. I'm taking my time to peruse them, stopping occasionally between whiffs of perfume samples to cut out images that catch my attention. It's rather soothing.

After a while, I have amassed a pile of images on the table in front of me, and it feels like a satisfying place to stop for now. I look at my collection and notice how similar many of the images are to each other. There's a lot of green and specifically a lot of plants. Plants in pots. A shelf with a few small succulents on it. A large tree in a terracotta planter standing in front of a wall of black-and-white, buffalo-checked wallpaper. Then, my eyes rest on one photo that is completely different from the others. It depicts what looks like a mobile of a bright orange sailboat hung to look like it's sailing through the air. I notice all the different colors, shapes, and patterns in the images and play with an arrangement that feels right. I glance at the clock and see that I've only got another fifteen minutes before we're supposed to gather to share what we've done, so I figure I better finish up.

But something doesn't feel right, and I freeze, still holding the glue in my hand. I can't bring myself to put the images on the canvas. I can't explain it, but something in my gut won't let me finish the collage. Instead, I set the clippings aside, and a different idea comes to mind. With the little time I have left, I pick up a brush and quickly create a painting that doesn't even have time to fully dry, which is what I bring to the group.

When we gather in the living room, Jenny, Jen, and Erna show their paintings and how they've captured different images of thriving amid patriarchy. Erna's is floral, bright, and colorful, with an image of a beautiful older woman at the center. Jenny's done two different paintings. One is somber in tone, and the other is full of flow and movement. Jen's is of the ocean with deep blues and greens. The group comments on each painting before the artist explains it to give everyone a chance to engage with what the art says to them. And then it's time to share mine. I hold it up.

My painting is stark and minimalistic—eight dark, broad strokes of paint run heavily across and down the canvas, almost like a grid. They dominate, but next to them, I tried adding some smaller bright pink spots in the in-between spaces. I don't get the shade quite right, and they look like splotches of blood. A mistake I tried unsuccessfully to fix sits in the upper-right-hand corner, and it looks like a small rectangle.

My friends take in what I've done. Jen says she thinks it's beautiful and intense. Jenny says the rectangle looks like a door. Erna notices how heavy the lines are. Someone says it reminds them of a prison.

I quickly realize how this stupid, fifteen-minute painting is hitting very close to home. It's as if the painting is asking me to admit how boxed in and small I feel right now. I sense some life, but what surrounds me feels like a prison. What's on the canvas does a better job of summing up how my soul feels than anything I can express through words. I'm in my forties; shouldn't I have figured out my life by now? I'm tempted to feel ashamed that my painting is so bleak, but I know my friends are in the pit with me. I decide that I agree with Jenny, and the little rectangle in the corner is a door. And it's time for me to use it. When I get home, I sign up for a coaching certification training that's happening in a couple months.

Moment Two

A Year and a Half Since the Dolphin Sighting

I'm connecting with Jessica, who is a strategic, thoughtful leader of a remarkable nonprofit organization that resources women and girls who are vulnerable to exploitation by giving them sustainable paths to employment. She is planning the annual team retreat and wants to take a day to help her team grow in self-awareness and communication and gain tangible tools to move forward. She wants to know if I would be interested in collaborating with her to facilitate the time. She doesn't use these words, but what I hear is, "Would you be interested in spending a day doing something that is exactly like your peak experiences and what makes you feel most alive with an incredibly talented team of people doing amazing work that aligns perfectly with what you said you wanted to do in your business?" I can't say yes fast enough.

After planning and preparation, the time arrives for the retreat. As I sit at my gate at the airport, my eyes focus on the door to the jet bridge, and I think of the escape door in my painting. My intuition tells me I'm about to walk through a divine threshold that's invisible to everyone but me.

The retreat turns out to be even better than I could have imagined. Facilitating the space for learning, dialogue, and insight with such a phenomenal team feels like pouring lighter fluid on the sparks of my aliveness. I'm grateful, satisfied, and proud of myself. As I make my way back to the airport, I think about how deeply life-giving it is to do something I feel made to do. To this day, I continue to value opportunities to engage with this incredible organization and many others that I'm honored to work with.

Moment Three

Three and a Half Years Since the Dolphin Sighting

During what was supposed to be a lazy Sunday afternoon, my husband has lost something he needs urgently. It's a storage drive of some sort, and he has to find a file on it for a project that's on deadline. It's not in any of the usual spots where he would typically put something like that, so now I'm helping him turn the house upside down to find it. We look in all the obscure corners, random drawers, and hidden boxes that haven't been touched in months, trying desperately to find this drive in a kind of deranged scavenger hunt. While I'm elbow-deep in random piles at the back of my closet, I find a small paper bag containing a stack of my children's baby clothes. My kids are older, so most of their baby things are long gone, but this is a small collection of items that were too precious to declutter.

When I reach into the bag, I feel a folded paper towel with something inside. As I take it out to look more closely, I realize it's a small stack of images, the clippings I couldn't put on the canvas that afternoon at the cabin. I must have shoved them in this bag when I unpacked and forgotten they were there. I immediately start to sob.

I'm crying tears of grief, remembering how low I was at that time in my life and how heavy the prison-like sadness and disappointment wore on me. I'm crying tears of gratitude, recognizing I'm not in that place anymore, and new doors have opened that allow me to do meaningful work I love. I'm crying tears of revelation, realizing that every desire I wanted in the VP role has come to be but in surprising ways I never predicted. I'm crying tears of recognition to see I now have space for those vibrant, green desires that didn't have a place on the canvas before. My desires had been speaking all along, and they'd been so wise. I'd heard their whispers, but I hadn't known the details of how they would inevitably make their way to me.

I decide it's time for these images to get a canvas. I lay them all out, bringing me back to the dining table at the cabin. I smile at the orange sailboat and imagine myself finding my way through that little escape door. I remember Jen, who has since passed away. I wish I could tell her how my desires and I are coming alive, and I wonder what she would say. Six months later, I start working full-time in my business with a roster of my dream clients.

Moment Four

Five Years Since the Dolphin Sighting

It's a random weekday, and I have several client calls, but I'm taking a few minutes before my next one to check my neighborhood Buy Nothing group. Even if I'm not looking for anything in particular, I like seeing people in the community giving and receiving everyday items. It warms my heart to see neighbors showing up for each other in this simple way; it's like a little booster shot for my faith in humanity.

Today, my neighbor has just posted some things to gift after a garage cleanout, and I stop scrolling to look more closely at one of the items that catches my attention: *Sailboat room decor: a bit dusty but still a cool piece, maybe for a kid's room.* The photos under the post are of a bright orange sailboat mobile. *That's so funny,* I think. *That reminds me of the bright orange sailboat mobile from my collage.*

I respond by saying I would love to have it, and since I'm the only interested party, my neighbor tells me it's mine. When the doorbell rings later, it's his son dropping it off for me via special delivery. I hold it up to look at it more closely. It's so pretty. It's a bit faded in a few places but is still a vibrant, beautiful shade of orange that reminds me of wild California poppies. It's worn, some of the sails need to be reglued in spots, and I see the dustiness my neighbor mentioned. I couldn't love it more.

Now I'm curious to compare this mobile with the one I remember, so I dig up the canvas from storage to see how similar they are. As I pull out the collage from a stack of papers, my jaw drops because the mobile is not just similar to the one I clipped from the magazine. It's an exact match. The mobile that was photographed and published in a magazine I came across and cut out five years ago is precisely the one that has just shown up at my house. The two-dimensional image just became real, and I'm holding it in my hands. I immediately text Jenny and Erna: *OMG, girls, you'll never believe what just showed up on my doorstep!*

This latest synchronicity is too weird and coincidental not to make me wonder why these moments keep happening. I mull this question over, looking for a satisfying answer.

I think of the journey I've been on that's littered with these moments. I remember deciding to put my name in the hat for the VP job. I recall my forty-day experiment and what it felt like when the dolphins appeared at the beach. I think about how thirty-five calls had me full-out dancing around my house. I consider the specific desires that have shown up in my notebooks time and time again. I look at everything that has happened since an unexpected rejection forced me to rethink what I knew about my desires, with all the disappointment, uncertainty, and beauty that come with them, and how it has formed a spiderweb of interconnected moments to create this story. It hits me—I always imagined that I was chasing my desires, but now I think they're chasing me back.

All along, my desires have been pursuing me to create divine alignment. I experience this deep alignment each time someone tells me that I've asked them a question they haven't considered on their own, or that I have given them the safe space, frameworks, and resources to grow. I feel this alignment when someone's face lights up because they understand their own story and experiences with greater clarity, and that insight helps them embrace their capacity for good, creativity, and leadership. I see purpose converging with desire when people tell me how they are making brave choices toward what they truly want. My desires keep chasing me, time and time again, nudging me to believe that my aliveness is meant to awaken aliveness in others.

I believe this is the way it works and that the divine responds to our desires with goodness, synchronicity, and abundance to unleash more magic in the world. Our desires chase us back, not just so we experience magic, but also so that we can make it.

The way you show up in the world is a beautiful response to living in profound connection with yourself, your desires, and others. When we align with our desires, we align with our true selves and our purpose. Listening to what you really want helps you discover how you can be of service to the world in your unique way. It gives you a way of offering something to the world that is authentic and dynamic, and it's very, very good for the people and communities that you love. Your desires are deeply personal, and they're also about much more.

When I lean in to listen to the universe, I hear a recurring tenor of celebration when people step into what they want. I detect the repeating notes of the surprising, the inevitable, and the satisfying in knowing our desires and the purpose that is born in them. It leads me to ask: What if what you want actually wants you back? And what if this is because the universe is ready to celebrate the magic that only you will bring?

Because if that's true, it changes the way we relate to our desires and the implications for our journey. The more that we have this awareness along the way, the more we can step into the embodiment of who our desires are helping us become.

If what you want actually wants you back, there's not just disappointment but also abundance in your desires.

The goodness of our desires is much more durable than rejection, heartbreak, and disappointment. Contrary to what we might be told, desires and disappointment are not one and the same. Disappointment is simply one aspect of what it means to live truer to what you want. Abundance also rises up and responds to your heart's desires. There's abundance waiting to meet you and bring your desires to life in beautiful, holistic, and reciprocal ways that will change you, your community, and the part of the world that you're meant to touch.

Learn to grapple with disappointment, but don't let it take over your imagination. Know that disappointment can be a thoughtful mentor as you learn to relate well to what you want. Remember why your desires are worth it. Be willing to be shaped by the same disappointment that makes most people abandon their desires and what's generative about them. Disappointment may be an unwelcome price to pay along the journey, but it isn't the final destination.

If what you want actually wants you back, the opportunities that are meant for you will find you.

Opportunities will come to you. Paths will clear. Doors will open. In fact, doors may open that you never conceived of on your own. You'll discover options, openings, and possibilities that fit your deepest desires.

Stay open to possibilities. Trust that things are making their way to you in both seen and unseen ways. Remember that you haven't yet seen all there is to see, and that the universe is bigger and more abundant than you know. Make the ask. Take the risk. Try. Be okay with making the leap and doing things scared. Be brave when you need to say no to the things that drain and deplete you because you know your desires will open the right opportunities that are made for you.

If you believe that what you want actually wants you back, rejection is protection.

Rejection stings, but when you believe that your desires actually want you back, you learn to see it as one of the highest forms of protection and redirection. It protects you from the things that you would have said yes to but would lead you farther away from your true self. It redirects you with a wisdom that you didn't yet have.

You do not need to have superhuman emotional armor in the face of rejection. Grieve and feel everything you need to feel. But remember that sometimes your desires are wiser than even you are about what truly aligns, and they will protect you. Know that there will be a day in the future when you'll look back and be able to wholeheartedly see the rejection as a blessing rather than a curse because of the way that it protected you, whether that day comes right away or not. When it does, you can say thanks for the grace of rejection.

If you believe that what you want actually wants you back, timelines aren't linear.

Time is relative, and especially so when it relates to your desires. Sometimes desires will appear more quickly than you could have imagined. Other times, much more slowly. Timelines won't always conform to your sensibilities about what they should be. But if you believe that what you want is finding its way to you, you can trust that your true desires will come to life at the right time and place.

Timing isn't something you can control. You can only control your responses and your actions, releasing the unknowable questions about how and when. Trust that your desires are not haphazard, and there is a thoughtfulness to their timing that is central to how they will come to be. Be patient when your desires are delayed a bit. Remember that it's more important to pay attention to the season you're in. Sometimes your soul will experience winter and quiet, and other times it will be spring and blooming. You'll learn to discern the difference. Be tenacious with the desires that have the biggest hold on your heart.

If you believe that what you want actually wants you back, you'll look for magic in your own story.

You may question whether magic is for you, or if it is just for other people. You may assume that setbacks mean you were being foolish to hope that there could be something more in your story, and it can feel like you're on your own with nothing else on your side.

Instead, have a keen eye for wonder, mystery, and magic each time it shows up in your life. Don't miss the signs that your desires will give you. Honor the synchronicities and find the meaning behind them. Take the symbols to heart, let them spark expectation, write them down, and hold them in your hands. Listen and relisten to the stories, the refrains, and the lyrics that resonate with the knowing in you. Be someone who looks for every Easter egg in your own story.

The Magic of Knowing What You Want

If you believe that what you want actually wants you back, you'll start to view knowing what you want as magical. Its magic leads you toward living a life marked by meaning, aliveness, imagination, curiosity, agency, and purpose. Your desires will show you the sacred, beautiful story of a life being knit together by you, deep and abiding abundance, and the divine.

We started this book by understanding desire fog and the partnership of purpose and desire. We continued by looking intently at who you've been made to be through the peak and contrast experiences that point to your unique brilliance, and we worked to uncover your aliveness. We stretched and expanded your capacity to imagine and believe possibilities could be there for you too. We planted this insight in the soil of your life through experimentation. We identified the outcomes and invitations that emerge as you integrate your being, your desires, and your story. The desires you have discovered have been unearthed from a profound intersection of being and becoming.

I want to give you one last invitation: Consider the possibility that as you're chasing your desires, you'll collect your own set of moments that will make you highly suspicious that your desires are also chasing you, that surprises will show up on your doorstep when you least expect it, and that you'll see how your aliveness brings something to the world that we need. One day, I hope you'll witness how what you want actually wanted you back all along. When these moments happen in your life, how you make sense of it is ultimately your call. Maybe you'll call it coincidence, but I like to call it magic.

There's magic in your desires. This magic doesn't involve spells, potions, or wands, but it's what happens when two types of magic collide—the magic of who you are and the magic of knowing what you want—giving rise to the magic you bring to the world. When that magic finds you and knocks on your door, it's the surprising, inevitable, satisfying conclusion you were looking for all along, and most important of all, it's just the beginning.

ACKNOWLEDGMENTS

I loved writing this book far more than anyone deserves. For the gift of this deep source of joy, I am forever grateful to the incredible humans without whom this would not exist.

First of all, I want to thank my clients and each person who has given me the honor of working together. Thank you for entrusting me with your honest emotions, questions, and beautiful stories. I am privileged to get to witness how each of you brings light to the world and am so inspired by you. Warmest thanks to those who have generously allowed parts of their story to be included here. I also want to offer special appreciation to those who were part of the Women Leading retreats and Authentic Alignment cohorts for being a part of conversations that helped these thoughts evolve.

Heartfelt gratitude to my agent, Ashley Hong, who brought her uncommon brilliance, experience, and drive to this project from day one. She possesses a genius for ideas and the written word that is such a delight to be around and she has a grace that makes working with her feel joyful and effortless.

She was there for the moments of elation and panic in every step of the process, and I'm indebted to her forever.

I would like to offer immense thanks to my editor, Grace P. Cho, who is a creative force of nature and whose encouragement inspired me to get serious about writing. To get to work with her has been one of the most meaningful collaborative experiences of my life. She's someone whose feedback is tough as nails but who manages to give it in a way that leaves you feeling seen and empowered to find your way forward, and I cannot envision a better guide to have in one's corner.

Sincere gratitude to the team at Revell, especially Olivia Peitsch, Eileen Hanson, Wendy Wetzel, Paula Gibson, and many others who contributed to shepherding this project through the publishing process. Thank you for believing in me. Warmest thanks to Lauren Cole and Joanna Ng for your sharp-eyed editorial support. A massive "thank you" to Derek Thornton of Notch Design and Illustration for the cover art.

I want to offer grateful acknowledgment to Tongua Williams, who helped me look for the presence of the sacred and created space for the inner journey of the writing process with compassion and clarity.

Enormous gratitude to Catherine Grooms, whose expertise and enduring support have helped me build my business as the dream job I didn't know I could create for myself, and who has always helped me listen to and trust myself.

Singular appreciation to the incredible individuals who endorsed the book: Dr. Peace Amadi, Kaitlin Curtice, Bora Reed, Jennifer Alvarez, Josh Green, Lashinda Demus, and Brian Chung. I respect and admire each of you and I'm truly humbled by your support.

All my love and thanks to the Busters, Jenny Hall and Erna Kim Hackett, for listening to me and walking alongside me through a grove of citrus trees when things fell apart. Your love, laughter, and deep wisdom have helped me rebuild my life. For that and hundreds of other ways, I know our friendship is one of the most significant treasures I have. Special remembrance of Jennifer Huerta Ball and gratitude for her.

To my family, I owe an immeasurable debt of gratitude to you. To my parents, Jin-Sheng and Teresa Shyr, thank you for your sacrifices and for being a source of support from the earliest days of my childhood and in every season of my life since. I'm proud to be your daughter. I'm grateful to the rest of my family: Alisa Leung, Raymond Leung, Riley Leung, Lauren Leung, Nicholas Leung, Raymond Gee, and my wonderful in-laws Cheuk and Emily Gee.

To my children, Marcus and Ryan, I'm grateful to be your mom. Learning who you are is one of my life's greatest joys and I'll love you forever. Thanks for being there as I wrote to be reminders of the importance of putting the work down for a moment to be present, play outside, or have dinner together. Ryan, thanks for being willing to step in as my ghostwriter. I'm not taking you up on it this time but I greatly appreciate the offer. Thank you to my godchildren, Lucy Hall, Tyler Hall, and Kayla Mammen, who genuinely inspire me when I think about the future.

I'm deeply grateful to my husband, Benny Gee, who vowed to love and support me a long time ago and has made good on that promise in a million ways, both in this process and in every other arena of life. I believe that when I look back on my life, one of the things I'll think of will be our morning walks spent talking about ideas, questions, and struggles in our lives, and how those times helped shape me to become who I'm meant to be. I'm so lucky that you're my person. Thank you for making me laugh out loud every day of these twenty-one years.

Lastly, thank you to my readers. I'm so grateful for your willingness to join in this conversation and I'm pulling for you.

NOTES

Chapter 1 What Do You Really Want?

1. NPR, "We Debate the Greatest TV Finales of All Time," *Pop Culture Happy Hour*, transcript, updated May 10, 2023, accessed October 30, 2023, https://www.npr.org/transcripts/1174267434.

Chapter 2 Purpose and Desire: A Tale of Two Siblings

1. Rick Warren, *The Purpose Driven Life: What on Earth Am I Here For?* (Grand Rapids: Zondervan, 2002), 21–22.

2. Teresa of Avila, *The Interior Castle*, trans. Kieran Kavanaugh and Otilio Rodriguez (New York: Paulist Press, 1979), 2–6.

3. Sonya Renee Taylor, *The Body Is Not an Apology: The Power of Radical Self-Love* (Berkeley: Berrett-Koehler Publishers, 2018).

4. Stephanie Buckhanon Crowder, *When Momma Speaks: The Bible and Motherhood from a Womanist Perspective* (Louisville: Westminster John Knox Press, 2006).

5. "What Is Restorative Justice?," Amplify RJ, accessed February 2023, https://www.amplifyrj.com/what-is-restorative-justice.

6. J. Michael Sparough, Jim Manney, and Tim Hipskind, *What's Your Decision? How to Make Choices with Confidence and Clarity* (Chicago: Loyola Press, 2010), 70–72.

7. Randy Woodley, *Becoming Rooted: One Hundred Days of Reconnecting with Sacred Earth* (Minneapolis: Broadleaf Books, 2022).

8. Aristotle, "Nicomachean Ethics," trans. W. D. Ross, in *The Complete Works of Aristotle: The Revised Oxford Translation*, ed. Jonathan Barnes (Princeton: Princeton University Press, 1984), 1744.

9. Parker J. Palmer, *Let Your Life Speak: Listening for the Voice of Vocation* (San Francisco: Jossey-Bass, 2000), 4.

Chapter 3 The Four Types of Questions That Get in the Way and What to Ask Instead

1. David Bredehoft, "The Science Behind Self-Affirmations," Psychology Today, August 7, 2023, https://www.psychologytoday.com/us/blog/the-age-of-overindulgence/202307/the-science-behind-self-affirmations.

2. Patrick Lencioni, *The 6 Types of Working Genius: A Better Way to Understand Your Gifts, Your Frustrations, and Your Team* (Dallas: Matt Holt Books, 2022), 181–3.

3. Tricia Hersey, *Rest Is Resistance: A Manifesto* (New York: Little, Brown Spark, 2022), 62.

4. Bronnie Ware, *The Top Five Regrets of the Dying: A Life Transformed by the Dearly Departing* (Carlsbad, CA: Hay House, 2012), 44–57.

5. Rainer Maria Rilke, *Letters to a Young Poet*, trans. Charlie Louth (London: Penguin Books 2011), 18.

Chapter 4 Stage One: Calibration

1. Gil Bailie, *Violence Unveiled: Humanity at the Crossroads* (New York: Herder & Herder, 2021), xv.

2. Jim Asplund, "How Your Strengths Set You Apart," Gallup CliftonStrengths, November 5, 2021, https://www.gallup.com/cliftonstrengths/en/356810/strengths-set-apart.aspx.

3. "Learn about the Science and Validity of Strengths," Gallup CliftonStrengths, accessed March 2024, https://www.gallup.com/cliftonstrengths/en/253790/science-of-cliftonstrengths.aspx.

4. Morgan Smith, "Harvard-Trained Neuroscientist: The 'Most Underrated' Skill Successful People Use at Work–and How to Develop It," CNBC, June 26, 2023, https://www.cnbc.com/2023/06/26/harvard-trained-neuroscientist-the-most-underrated-skill-successful-people-use-at-work.html.

Chapter 5 Stage Two: Expansion

1. Robin Wall Kimmerer, *Braiding Sweetgrass: Indigenous Wisdom, Scientific Knowledge, and the Teachings of Plants* (Minneapolis: Milkweed Editions, 2013), 3–10.

2. Laura Vanderkam, *168 Hours: You Have More Time Than You Think* (New York: Portfolio, 2010), 40–45.

Chapter 6 Stage Three: Experimentation

1. Bill Burnett and Dave Evans, *Designing Your Life: How to Build a Well-Lived, Joyful Life* (New York: Alfred A. Knopf, 2016), xxvi.

Chapter 7 Stage Four: Integration

1. Weilian Wang, "Sai Weng Lost His Horse," trans. James Legge, in *The Chinese Classics: Volume II—The Works of Mencius*, ed. James Legge, *Sacred Books of the East*, vol. 16 (Oxford: Clarendon Press, 1895), 271–2.

2. J.S. Park, *As Long as You Need: Permission to Grieve* (Nashville: Thomas Nelson, 2024), Spotify ed., 8:22, https://open.spotify.com/show/3VFmxGL0IMqlrdsO6jvKLJ?si=c229aa30c2d3474a.

Chapter 8 The How-Tos of Desire-Based Goal Setting

1. Richard Batts, "Why Most New Year's Resolutions Fail," Ohio State University, Fisher College of Business, February 2, 2023, https://fisher.osu.edu/blogs/leadreadtoday/why-most-new-years-resolutions-fail#:~:text=Researchers%20suggest%20that%20only%209,by%20the%20end%20of%20January.

2. George T. Doran, "There's a S.M.A.R.T. Way to Write Management Goals and Objectives," *Management Review* 70, no. 11 (1986): 35–36.

3. Angela Duckworth, *Grit: The Power of Passion and Perseverance* (New York: Scribner, 2016), 91.

4. "Beat Stress with Science," transcript, Zoe.com, updated April 10, 2024, accessed March 12, 2024, https://zoe.com/learn/podcast-beat-stress-with-science.

TRACEY GEE is a certified leadership coach and consultant dedicated to guiding individuals toward transformative self-awareness and meaningful personal and professional growth. As an author, Tracey draws insight from her extensive experience across workshops, speaking engagements, and personalized coaching sessions. Her diverse clientele includes UC Berkeley, Firm Foundation, AltaMed, Nomi Network, Coca-Cola, Amazon, and the Miami Heat. She is a certified facilitator in four

frameworks—Gallup CliftonStrengths, Working Genius, Enneagram, and Cultural Intelligence. Tracey is originally from the Bay Area of California and now lives in Los Angeles with her husband, children, and dog, Kona. She loves coffee shops and every dog she's ever met.

CONNECT WITH TRACEY
or book her for a speaking engagement

TraceyGee.me   TraceyGee.me

Facebook.com/TraceyGeeLLC   LinkedIn.com/TraceySGee

TraceyGee.me

Dear Reader,

Thank you for selecting a Revell book! We're so happy to be part of your life through this work.

Revell's mission is to publish books that offer hope and help for meeting life's challenges, and that bring comfort and inspiration. We know that the right words at the right time can make all the difference; it is our goal with every title to provide just the words you need.

We believe in building lasting relationships with readers, and we'd love to get to know you better. If you have any feedback, questions, or just want to chat about your experience reading this book, please email us directly at publisher@revellbooks.com. Your insights are incredibly important to us, and it would be our pleasure to hear how we can better serve you.

We look forward to hearing from you and having the chance to enhance your experience with Revell Books.

The Publishing Team at Revell Books
A Division of Baker Publishing Group
publisher@revellbooks.com